# Post-Colonialism, Subalterns and Community

*By the Same Author*

1. Christian Ethics: Issues & Insights
2. Contextual Issues: Theological, Ethical and Missiological Responses
3. Human Rights: Concepts and Perspectives
4. Introducing Post Modernism and Post Colonialism

---

**About the Author**

**Rev. Dr. M. Stephen** hails from Kottayam (Kerala, India) is a writer, orator and author. He has authored around 30 books in Malayalam and English. He received his B.A. and M.A. (in English Literature) from Kerala University, B.D. (UBS, Pune) and M.Th. (UTC, Bangalore) from Serampore University (West Bengal), and Doctorate from Dharmaram Vidyakshetram : Pontifical Athenaeum of Philosophy and Theology, Bangalore. He is a theological teacher and teaches theology and ethics at Faith Theological Seminary, Manakala, Adoor, Kerala. The famous publishers such as 'Concept', 'Serials' and ISPCK have published his books. 'Human Rights', 'Contextual Issues', 'Christian ethics : Issues and Insights, and introducing post-modernism and post-colonialism are published by Concept Publishing Company Pvt. Ltd., New Delhi.

# POST-COLONIALISM, SUBALTERNS AND COMMUNITY

Rev. M. Stephen

CONCEPT PUBLISHING COMPANY PVT. LTD.
NEW DELHI-110059

**ISBN-13: 978-93-5125-167-5**

First Published 2015

*Published and Printed by*

Concept
Since 1974

**Concept Publishing Company Pvt. Ltd.**
A/15-16, Commercial Block, Mohan Garden
New Delhi-110059 (India)
*T*: 25351460, 25351794, *F*: 091-11-25357109
E: publishing@conceptpub.com, W: www.conceptpub.com
**Editorial Office:** H-13, Bali Nagar, New Delhi-110 015, India.

Cataloging in Publication Data--Courtesy: D.K. Agencies (P) Ltd. <docinfo@dkagencies.com>

Sttīphan, Em., author.
Post-colonialism, subalterns and community / Rev. M. Stephen.
pages cm
Includes index.
ISBN 9789351251675

1. Marginality, Social--India. 2. Postcolonialism--India. I. Title.

DDC 305.560954 23

# Contents

# Contents

# Introduction

The most struggling people in the world are the Subalterns or the marginalized. They are the powerless and the dehumanized people. They may include the poor, *dalits*, tribes, victimized women, blacks, fisherfolk, transgenders and the slum-dwellers. Their emancipation is key to progress and development. But it is so happened that they are being oppressed in the name of the development by the powerful.

It is also important to look at the community that we develop. Today, community has become an inclusive and broader concept. It is not very static, but dynamic. Civil society is also a community which can be even a global community, which include the cyber community. The 'community' transcends religious, ideological, caste and class barriers. They also stand for common good and for development of a human society.

The post-colonial ideological framework can help us to overcome the colonial, imperial and the oppressive spirit which challenges the identity, dignity and the rights of the Subaltern. An indigenous, liberative and non-pyramidal perspective is found in post-colonialism. It is deconstructive and empowering.

This book, 'Post-colonialism, Subalterns and Community' deals with the issues of the alienated and voiceless people who are in need of empowerment. Hope this book would help us to open our eyes to the reality and to involve in the mission of humanization.

**Rev. Dr. M. Stephen**

# 1
# Post-colonialism and Subaltern Identity
## A Theoretical and Philosophical Framework

Post-colonialism is a state or condition like Post-modern condition (Lyotard) and it is also a perspective, ideology and attitude. The post-colonial thinking was found even before the colonial era ended. Anti-colonialism is a protest or resistance against colonialism, and post-colonialism is an ideology and theory. Post-colonialism has a romance about the past—the precolonial era. From the philosophical perspective, post-colonialism is a worldview which challenges the colonial, imperial and domineering spirits and ideologies that enslaves us.

### Post-modernism and Post-colonialism

People used to ask questions regarding the difference between post-modernism and post-colonialism. These two ideologies have different starting points. Post-modernism is a reaction to modernism and post-colonialism is a response to colonialism.

Though 'deconstruction' is used in post-colonialism, it is strictly related to Jacque Derrida's post-structural linguistic analysis. In post-colonialism, the reaction is 'decolonize'. Both these concepts are, however, related and that is why Spivak, the post-colonial thinker is referred as Marxist deconstructivist thinker. Post-colonialism is interested in the re-writing of history, ideologies and text-books which are written by dominant groups from their euro-centric or elitistic perspective which disregarded and dehumanized the identity of the subalterns. Post-colonialism also asserts the re-reading of the sacred texts which affirms hierarchy, casteism, patriarchy, apartheid and other forms of injustices and discriminations. There is de-legitmation of what is Western and dominant in post-colonialism. The de-legitimation is also found in deconstruction in post-modernism.

Post-modernism is also a culture and ideology and condition. Post-colonialism and post-modernism affirm the deconstruction, delegimation, pluralism, contextuality and liberation. Post-modernism supports indeterminacy, anomie, and absolute relativism which are not very much affirmed by post-colonialism. The role of God in history is also important in post-colonial thinking. We also see 'a/moral' dimensions in post-modernism (Foucault). The 'a/moral' and 'a/God' dimensions are related to post-modernism and not to post-colonialism. But, it is important to note that the questions of the marginalized or subalterns are taken care by post-modernism (e.g. Foucault) and post-colonialism. Post-modernism and post-colonialism do challenge the grand/meta-narratives and pyramidal structures raised by modernism and colonialism. Any centrism which is authoritarian and despotic are anti-people to post-modernism and post-colonialism.

The post-colonial elements such as decentering and anti-hierarchical and anti-pyramidal are found in Pentecostal movement, especially in new generation churches. There is a subaltern origin to pentecostal movement in United States as William Joseph Seymour was the leader of Azusa Street (1906) revival. He was an Afro-American. The Indian pentecostal movement is also largely a subaltern movement. The Christians in India are also mostly belonging to Subaltern groups. Pentecostalism was challenging the hierarchical or monolithic societal and Church structures.

### The Question of Subaltern Identity

'Subaltern' means 'inferior rank'. It means a person who belongs to the margins or periphery. Antonio Gramsci, the Italian Marxist thinker used the term 'Subaltern' to refer the 'proletariat' or the labour class. It means the marginalized.

There was a growing subaltern consciousness in the twentieth century as the question of the aboriginals, natives and the marginated groups or oppressed ones are taken seriously. They were sidelined in history for many centuries and their role, status, dignity, rights and identity are denied. In the Indian context, the sociologist Ranajit Guha and others have shown interest in Subaltern studies. The poor, slum-dwellers, *dalits*, tribes, victimized women, victimized children, transgenders, sex workers, fisherfolk and the indigenous groups of people are the Subalterns as they are oppressed. Their social mobility is restricted by the dominant forces. In India, the Brahminic and other dominant forces have ideologically, physically and psychologically oppressed the powerless. The empowerment and the emancipation of the powerless or the subalterns is very important.

The identity is constructed by the dominant groups to dehumanize others. The 'lower caste' identity is ascribed to some groups of people of India by the Brahmin forces is an example for this. Identity is related to ethnicity, religion, ideology and socio-economic status. All identities are in a move to emerge. The *dalits*, tribes, transgenders and the women are trying to emerge and trying to affirm their new identity in the context of oppression, victimization and dehumanization. In India, the identity of the *dalits*, tribes and the victimized women are in a threat. The rights and dignity are integral to identity which are questioned as they are forcefully evacuated from their habitat as their status is recognized as 'no people' and landless. The women are also sexually assaulted as they are considered as objects by the male-chauvinistic society. The girl children are also victims of forced labour and sexual violence.

The 'construct' of an identity by the dominant groups to dehumanize others is a distortion. Every person has a 'self' and that selfhood or identity has to be regarded. That identity is based on equality, justice and freedom. Post-colonialism challenges the low status that is ascribed to some groups of people, especially the indigenous people, to dehumanize them. The colonial forces did not recognize the dignified identity of the colonized natives, and now the local elites or dominant forces are denying the same to the indigenous groups, poor and marginalized. This is the paradox that we are confronting.

What is post-colonial is that it challenges the indignity that is ascribed to the identities. The colonial and neo-colonial forces are at work to question the identity of the subalterns. The Euro-centric and local dominant forces are at work in this process. The social movements are at work in order to curb the work of the dominant forces. The Narmada Valley Struggle, the Chengara Struggle (Pathanamthitta district, Kerala), the land struggle under the leadership of C.K. Janu (Gothra Sabha), in Wynad (Kerala), and the resistance by the tribes in Niyamgiri (Odisha) against Bauxite mining by Vedanta and Posco are the examples for this. There are also other social movements based on ecological (e.g. chipko), *dalit* and tribal issues.

## Re-imaging of Philosophy and Theology

The Western theologies are oriented mostly in Western philosophy, economics, sociology and culture. They may also have a domineering and colonial spirit. They are elitistic in nature. The Western framework is also very abstract, which is uncritically used by theologians in their formulations. Western philosophies are highly based on natural law, hierarchical in nature, so they affirm gradations and discriminations as they are rooted in natural orders, which deny the value and diginity of the marginated like *dalits*, tribes, blacks, women, children and the labour class. They are not concerned of people who live in ghettoes, who are subalterns. This nature of philosophy is also reflected in Western theologies. Experiences of the poor are not considered in Western philosophies and theologies. Most of the empirical realities are ignored by them.

The philosophies and theologies of the West have developed a 'system' which is classical, closed, and abstract which is challenged by post-modernism and post-colonialism. Deconstruction became the key word in re-imaging philosophies and theologies. The existing parameters of 'knowledge' and theories are being questioned. The subaltern consciousness has impacted to have a new understanding on realities. The feminism, *dalit* and tribal awakening have created a new awareness in theology. The worldviews, experiences, traditions and expression of the maginated groups are considered in theologizing today. The voices of the victimised, the sufferings of Third World people, their culture and socio-political experience are a great concern in theology today. The subaltern, victimized and oppressed are the 'other' who are powerless, who are to be the central concern in our theologizing.

There is epistemological shift as we see the influence of post-modernism and post-colonialism. The authorities and traditions are undergoing challenges. The reason is replaced by experience especially of the subalterns. The elitistic traditions like the Brahminic and Western are also being challenged by the subalterns. The sources of authority are now considered from the *dalits*, tribes, blacks and other victimized groups. Their historical consciousness and traditions, religiosity, culture and experiences are considered as very valuble and they are very much used in the making of theology. A de-legitimation or deconstruction or decolonizing is taking place in every sphere. The monolithic structures, ideologies philosophies and theologies are undergoing criticism as they are not considering the issues of the context and people. The classical form of epsistemology is being challenged by the people from margins. The dominant class and their views and pre-suppositions are questioned by the marginalized.

## Post-Colonial Philosophy

Post-colonial philosophy affirms the end of colonialism which subjugates, exploits and oppresses the colonized countries by the

Western powers. Post-colonialism views a world or a country which is free politically and economically. The Post-colonial era is a radical departure from the hegemonic powers. Post-colonial life is one of independent and liberated. The aggressive imperial powers have regulated once the life of the colonized, and colonizers have imposed their 'superiority' and authority over the colonized. The Western powers have used not only political power, but also used all subtle means to dominate the people of the colonies.

The colonial powers have questioned the value and importance of traditional or indigenous knowledge. They also rejected the potentiality of the native people. The colonial powers always claim that they have more intelligence than the colonized. They also claim that their theories, perspectives and arguments are superior than the natives. The colonial powers have also claimed racial superiority. They also think that their view of life and habits are better than the colonized people. The colonial powers also have the perspective that their religious beliefs and practices are superior. These claims and perspectives of the colonial powers are being radically challenged by post-colonialism.

Hybridity is an important subject in post-colonialism. In McLeod's words, the subject becomes produced from the process of hybridisation. A person's subjectivity is composed from various sources, different materials, many locations—demolishing for ever the idea of subjectivity as stable, single or 'pure' (John McLeod, *Beginning postcolonialism*, New Delhi: Viva Books, 2010. p. 219). It is also stated, 'The concept of hybridity has proved very important for diaspora peoples, and indeed many others too, as a way of thinking beyond exclusionary, fixed, binary notions of identity based on ideas of rootedness and cultural, racial and national purity. Hybrid identities are never total and complete in themselves, like ordinary pathways but from crazy-paving. Instead, they remain perpetually in motion, pursuing errant and unpredictable routes, open to change and reinscription' (*Ibid*, p. 219). In hybridity 'new ethnicities' and new identities can be created. Multi-culturalism and multi-ethnicity are related to this hybridity. Cultural diversity and pluralism are part of hybridity (*Ibid.,* p. 225, 227). It also creates a transnational forms of community (*Ibid.*, p. 231).

Post-colonial philosophy affirms the value of indigenous religion, culture, wisdom and way of life. It also upholds the identity and dignity of native people. Colonial philosophy is to subjugate, to rule over and even to annihilate the indigenous people. Post-colonialism draws our attention to the insensible and inhuman approach which is found in colonial philosophy. The colonial philosophy was to annihilate native people to control them or mix with them (by illicit sexual contact or by marriage). The last method was widely applied in certain countries by which there is a confusion about the new race. By using this method, the colonizers bring confusion over the native people. By this means the identity of native people became a confused identity. Philosophy is a view of life. The colonial philosophy is to use all deceptive means to dominate the colonized people and to tap their energy and resources, and to enslave them. This spirit of domineering is challenged by post-colonialism. Post-colonial philosophy affirms what is native or indigenous and contextual and it is liberative. Post-colonialism promotes nationalism and nation-building.

## The Important Post-Colonial Thinkers

### *(a) Edward Said*

His famous book is 'Orientalism'. He is understood as an originator of post-colonial discourse theory. Post-colonialism deals with impact of European conquest on colonized societies. It deals with political struggle and cultural struggle. There is an impact of language also on colonised societies. One of the example from the ancient past is the hellenization of Greeks. English, French, Latin and Spanish languages are imposed on colonized countries by the Western countries.

Edward Said talks about the worldliness of the text as text is located in the world. For Said, 'a text, in its actually being a text, is being in the world', states Bill Ashcroft and Paul Ahluwalia (*Edward Said,* London: Routledge, 2007. p. 21). In Said's opinion, texts announce their materiality, their worldliness by their situatedness in just the same way as speech (*Ibid.*, p. 22). In the post-colonial societies, there is dominance of colonial languages. In most of the colonial societies, they are speaking some one's language and not theirs. Said states, the languages in which we are speaking is his before it is mine'. Looking at the possibilities of critical reading Edward Said suggests 'affiliation' which is a process of identification through culture which is closer to worldliness of text, than filiation which refers to lines of descent in nature or heritage. For him, states Ashcroft and Ahluwalia, 'an affiliative reading allows the critic to see the literary work as a phenomenon in the world, located in a network of non-literary, non-canonical and non-traditional affiliations' (*Ibid.*, p 25).

Affiliation is understood as a feature of text's worldliness. Affiliation enables the text to maintain itself as a text, the status of the author, historical moment, conditions of publication, diffusion and reception, values drawn upon and values and ideas assumed. Affiliation draws us to the location and locatedness of the text's production (*Ibid.*, pp. 25-26). According to Ashcroft and Ahluwalia, "For Edward Said the world from which the text originated, the world with which it was affiliated, was crucial, not only for the business of interpretation but also for its ability to make an impact on readers" (*Ibid.*, p. 27).

According to Ashcroft and Ahluwalia, "Orientalism, in Said's formulation, is principally a way of defining and 'locating' Europe's others. But as a group of related disciplines, orientalism was, in important ways, about Europe itself, and hinged on arguments that circulated around the issue of national distinctiveness, and racial and linguistic origins" (*Ibid.*, pp. 50-51). The word 'orient' refers to the colonies, for the British and the French. But for Americans, it refers to far East, especially Japan and China (*Ibid.*, p. 57). His one way of defining orientalism as a corporate institution is demonstrative of its amorphous capacity as a structure used to dominate and authorize the orient. This view is linked to colonialism (*Ibid.*, p. 57).. According to Edward Said, the power of the orientalists lay in their 'knowing' the orient, which in itself constituted power and yet also was an exercise in power (*Ibid.*, p. 68).

While summarizing Edward Said's understanding on 'orientalism', Ashcroft and Ahluwalia stated, "the essence of Said's argument is that to know something is to have power over it and conversely, to have power is to be able to know the world in your own terms. When this something is a whole region of the world in which dozens of ethnicities, nationalities and languages are gathered under the spurious category the orient, then the link between that knowledge and the power it confirms becomes profoundly important" (*Ibid.*, p. 83).

In Edward Said's book 'culture and imperialism', he talks about the imperial culture which justify and reinforce the establishment and exploitation of empire, and the other is countering this idea, that is the historical experience of resistance against empire (*Ibid.*, p. 87). Imperial culture is the most powerful instrument of imperial hegemony (*Ibid.*, p. 88). For Said, imperialism is the practice, theory, and attitude of dominating metropolitan centre ruling a distant territory. Colonialism, for him, is implanting of settlements on a distant territory (*Ibid.*, p. 90). In order to understand the imperial presence in text, Said suggest the contrapuntal reading. It is explained as a form of 'reading back' from the perspective of the colonised, to show how the submerged but crucial presence of the empire emerges in canonical texts. As we begin to read, not univocally but contrapuntally, with a simultaneous awareness of both of the metropolitan history and other subjected and concealed histories against which the dominant discourse acts and we obtain a different sense of what is going on in the text (*Ibid.*, p. 92).

According to Ashcroft and Ahluwalia, "Contrapuntal reading is a technique of theme and variation by which a counterpoint is established between the imperial narrative and the post-colonial perspective, a 'counter-narrative, that keeps penetrating beneath the surface of the individual texts to elaborate the ubiquitous presence of imperialism in canonical culture" (*Ibid.*, p. 93). The both dimensions of polyphony is considered by contrapuntal reading. Said talks about two phases of decolonisation: (1) Recovery of geographical territory, and (2) 'Changing of cultural territory'. The primary resistance involves fighting against outside intrusion, and the secondary resistance entails ideological or cultural reconstitution. For Said, resistance is a process in the rediscovery and repatriation of what had been suppressed in the natives' past by the process of imperialism (*Ibid.*, p. 108). Said describes negritude as a nativist phenomenon which linked with anti-colonial stances (*Ibid.*, p. 110).

### *(b) Gayatri Chakravorty Spivak (1942)*

It is observed, "Gayatri Chakravorty Spivak is best known for her overtly political use of contemporary cultural and critical theories to challenge the legacy of colonialism on the way we read and think about literature and culture. What is more, Spivak's critical interventions encompass a range of theoretical interests, including Marxism, Feminism, deconstruction, post-colonial theory and cutting-edge work on globalisation" (Stephen Morton, *Gayatri Chakravorty Spivak*, London: Routledge: 2007). Gayatri Spivak was born in Calcutta (India), and did her early education in India. She had her higher education in the West. Her works include, 'the post-colonial critic' and 'a critique of post-colonial reason'. According to Stephen Morton, Spivak has foregrounded the textual elements that shape our understanding of the social world and where by questioned the binary opposition between philosophical or literary texts and the so called real world (*Ibid.*, p. 4). In the words of Morton, 'Spivak exposes how the world is represented from the dominant perspective and geopolitical location of the 'First world' to the exclusion of other disenfranchised groups' (*Ibid.*, p. 5). She was critical of the historian of subaltern studies who used Marxian methodology.

She was emphasizing, Morton states, that western Marxist model of social change that these historians employ does not do justice to the complex histories of subaltern insurgency and resistance that they seek to recover (*Ibid.*, p. 7). She had the opinion that the complex life of Third World women cannot be properly represented by the vocabulary of western critical theory (*Ibid.*, p. 7).

Spivak was anxious about the fact that Indian nationalism has failed to emancipate the lower class, subaltern women. According to Morton the argument of Spivak is that before we can learn anything about the economic text of globalisation or the patriarchal oppression of Third World women, we must first unlearn the privileged system of Western knowledge that have indirectly served the interests of colonialism and neo-colonialism (*Ibid.*, p. 9). Talking about the development of World Bank and World Trade Organization, Spivak refers that this dominant representation of the world as 'worlding', or the assumption that when the colonizers came to the world, they encounter it as uninscribed earth upon which they write their inscriptions (*Ibid.*, p. 18). According to Morton, "the term 'worlding in Spivak's work refers to the way in which writing in general, or textuality, has provided a rhetorical structure to justify imperial expansion" (*Ibid.*, p. 19). It is stated by Morton that at times Spivak uses the term epistemic violence to emphasize how Western knowledge or epistemology has been used to justify the violent exercise of political and military force over other non-Western cultures (*Ibid.*, p. 19). Spivak was referred by Colin Mac Cabe as a 'Feminist Marxist deconstructivist'. According to Morton, "For Spivak, the 'political' value of a deconstructive reading practice is that it guards against the universal claims of Marxism, national liberation movements or Western feminism to speak for all the oppressed" (*Ibid.*, p. 35).

Spivak was critical of the Western feminists for ignoring the specific experiences of 'Third World' women when they construct a universal feminist subject, states Morton (*Ibid.*, p. 40). In Spivak we can see the influence of Derrida's deconstruction in the development of post-colonial thought. In the words of Stephen Morton, the experience of disempowered subaltern groups in the post-colonial world present an ethical dilemma as well as a methodological challenge to Spivak. Her writings also demonstrate the experience of social and political oppression in post-colonial societies such as India cuts across differences in class, region, language ethnicity, religion, generation, gender and citizenship (*Ibid.*, p. 46). Spivak, states Morton, emphasizes that the classical Marxist methodology of the subaltern studies collective prevents them from reading the histories of women's resistance in India (*Ibid.*, p. 47). Spivak also has the opinion that the subaltern women are silenced by British colonization and the Hindu patriarchal spirit (*Ibid.*, p. 64).

One of Spivaks contribution, States Morton, is that she demands that feminism should consider seriously the material histories and lives of 'Third World' women in its account of women's struggle against oppression (*Ibid.*, p. 71). In her view on subaltern women, she challenges the universal claims of feminism to speak for all women (*Ibid.*, p. 71). For her, it is not adequate to speak for all women as Western feminists do regardless of cultural difference, states Morton (*Ibid.*, p. 78). Spivak challenges the universal humanist assumption that all women's lives and histories are the same. She also stresses the importance of global political awareness of the local Economic, Political, Social and Cultural conditions that structure women's oppressions in different parts of the world (*Ibid.*, p. 91).

According to Stephen Morton, 'Spivak's engagement with post-colonial texts is motivated in part by a desire to challenge the totalizing system of subaltern agency or resistance' (*Ibid.*, p. 123). She is also critical of the political promises of Third World nationalism and decolonisation, especially from the perspective of subaltern women and the underclass (*Ibid.*, p. 124). She was quite aware of the domineering elements in nationalism. She argues, states Morton, that post-colonial nationalism is divided between the state political programmes of ruling governmental elites and the popular struggles of the people who are often ignored by the dominant political programmes (*Ibid.*, p. 124). For her, if history is written from the perspective of the struggles of the marginated (e.g., popular struggles and peasant rebellions) that literature can provide a rhetorical space for subalterns to re-articulate the suppressed histories of people's struggles (*Ibid.*, p. 124). Spivak was suggesting an ethics of reading which is more sensitive to the location of subaltern women, says Morton. She argues for the notion of ethics as a responsibility of the self (Western) to the other (non-Western).

Gayatri Chakravorty Spivak was known as a post-colonial critic, and she was very cautious of the nationalism and post-colonial thinking which fail to consider the situation and the struggles of the subaltern. She was very much influenced by post-modern thinking, especially of the Deconstruction of Derrida.

### *(c) Homi K. Bhabha (1949)*

He was born in a Parsi community in Bombay. At present he is teaching English and American literature at Harvard University. He provides a working theory of cultural hybridity. For him, the new internationalism is a history of post-colonial migration, the narratives of cultural and political diaspora and the major social displacements of peasants and aboriginal communities (*The Location of Culture,* London: Routledge classics, 1994. p. 7). So Bhabha states that the concepts such as homogeneous national cultures, consensual transmission of historical traditions or 'organic' ethnic communities are in need of redefinition (*Ibid.*, p. 7). He also states, "Post-coloniality, for its part, is a salutary reminder of the persistent 'neo-colonial' relations within the 'new' world order and the multinational division of labour. Such a perspective enables the authentication of histories of exploitation and the evolution of strategies of resistance" (*Ibid.*, p. 9).

Bhabha explains the 'hybridity' as follows: "Private and public, past and present, the psyche and the social develop an interstitial intimacy. It is an intimacy that questions binary divisions through which such spheres of social experiences are often spatially opposed. These spheres of life are linked though an 'in-between' temporality that takes the measure of dwelling at home, while producing an image of the world history. This is the moment of aesthetic distance that provides the narrative with a double edge, which like the coloured South African subject represents a hybridity, a difference 'within', a subject that inhabits the rim of an 'in-between' reality (*Ibid.*, p. 9). The South African coloured is affected by displacement, exile or diaspora and living in ghettoes which are 'unhomely' situations.

Bhabha talks also about the importance of hybrid moment of political change. He argues for the negotiation between gender and class. For him, the transformational value of change lies in the rearticulation, or translation, of elements that are neither the one unitary working class, nor the other (the politics of gender) but something else besides which contests the terms and territories of both (*Ibid.*, p. 41). Hybridity, for him is not unifying the elements, but to have negotiations with them. He argues along with Stuart Hall, the construction of a counter hegemonic power block which consists of unemployed, semi-skilled and unskilled, part-time workers, male and female, the low paid, black people, underclass. It is a structure of heterogeneity, signs of fragmentation of class and cultural consensus which is related to historical experience of contemporary social division. This kind of hybridity is used as a political alternative. It can be also called the principle of political negotiation (*Ibid.*, p. 41).

Entering into the 'Third space' is the context of international culture or diversity of cultures where, Bhabha says, the articulation of culture's hybridity (*Ibid.*, p. 56). According to him, this Third space has a colonial or post-colonial provenance. Bhabha states, 'we should remember that it is the 'inter'—the cutting edge of translation and negotiation, the in-between space—that carries the burden of the meaning of culture. It makes it possible to begin envisaging national, anti-nationalist histories of the, 'people'. And by exploring this Third space, we may elude the politics of polarity and emerge on the others of ourselves' (*Ibid.*, p. 56).

The indigenous traditions engage in post-colonial struggle against the dominant relations of power and knowledge states Bhabha. It may sound that Bhabha's view of hybridity is a post-colonial discussion in his own way, and not strictly anti-colonial and anti-hegemonic. His approach takes a middle position to integrate the opposites which is found in politics in the form of negotiations. It is also to be noted that some of the so called prominent postcolonial thinkers live in the West and formed post-colonial theories, philosophies and theologies using the Western resources theories and methods, which are not quite suiting to the Third World situation (i.e., the victimized or marginated people and their struggles). A radical departure from the colonial/hegemonic powers is inevitable. A movement towards indignity (appreciation of what is native), contextuality and liberative spirit is essential for post-colonial approach. And post-colonialism should not be a space for any kind of arbitrary discussions.

Bhabha was concerned of the site of culture which is temporal. According to him, cultural differences must not be understood as the free play of polarities in the homogeneous empty time of the national community, but it is the jarring of meanings and values generated in the process of cultural interpretation as an effect of the perplexity of living in the liminal spaces of national society (*Ibid.*, p. 232).

## Post-Colonial Hermeneutics

Post-colonialism challenges the colonial notions and perspectives. In colonialism, the 'other' is not important, but in post-modernism and post-colonalism there is re-imagining or reviewing of the perspective on the other. The other is the marginated ones who play significant roles in history. The post-structural/post-modern elements like deconstruction or delegitmation is found in post-colonial interpretation. The aspects like orientalism, contrapuntal, hybridity are very much stressed by certain post-colonial thinkers in their interpretation. The post-colonial hermeneutics has to identify the oppressive and dehumanizing elements and resist and re-interpret them. The oppressive elements are found as it finds them in the dominant, elitistic, Western and colonial interpretations. The post-colonial hermeneutics should have the following characteristics:

(1) It is post-structural. Post-colonial reading is post-structural in character. The texts can have 'meaning' beyond the meaning. Here the post-modernism also play on important role, as the text is to be re-structured or deconstructed. The colonial reading which is distorted and oppressive has to be deconstructed. Here the reader play a vital role in the re-reading. Post-colonial reading is a challenge to the structures of domination. Post-colonial hermeneutics focuses on identifying the structures which projects and supports the imperial, dominant or oppressive spirit and to resist and de-legitimize them. The counter elements or what is contrapuntal or resisting the colonial spirit is also very crucial here.

(2) It is contextual or indigenous in character. The principle of contextuality plays a significant role in post-colonial hermeneutics. Post-colonialism is a resistance to colonialism and its thinking. The decolonizing process is coming back to the roots. It affirms the nativity or indignity. The spirit of indignity or contextuality is found in Third World hermeneutices and theology. Asian/Indian and Latin American theologies and hermeneutics consider the contextuality very seriously. It recognizes the experiences, values, historical struggles of the oppressed and colonized humanity. Biblical text has to be interpreted not on the basis of imported or Western ideology and theology, but on the basis of the contextual experiences of the people. It has to consider the socio-economic and political reality of the oppressed or colonized people.

(3) There is liberative character in post-colonial hermeneutics. It challenges or critically looks at the

colonial and oppressive structures. It goes against the tides. It challenges the legitimization of the oppression and domination. It is conflictual in nature. It has dissenting voice against injustice and exploitation. It sides the marginelized like poor, *dalits*, tribes, blacks victimized women and other oppressed or subaltern groups. It is a dynamic process in the interpretation of the scripture. Scripture is interpreted with a liberative motif, as it recognizes the struggle of the oppressed. It also considers the historical and sociological realities. The aspect of liberation is found in the Third World reading of the text. Feminist, *dalit*, tribal and black and other liberative hermeneutics considers the importance of radical restructuring in the concepts, structures value system and perspectives. It aims at the liberation.

According to C.I. David Joy the post-colonial analysis of the text reading will expose the following:

(1) The colonial motifs hidden in text.
(2) The colonial intentions of the interpreters of the text.
(3) An alternative way for monologic reading.
(4) Native cultures as they are taken into account.
(5) Reading as it becomes a gesture of resistance ('Historical Jesus Research: A Post-colonial Cultural Reconstruction', *Bangalore Theological Form*, Vol. XLI, No. 2, (December 2009), p. 88). David Joy also quotes from the article "Biblical criticism and post-colonial studies" by Fernando Segovia, who talks about three foci which are to be noted in the process of post-colonial reading. They are as follows:
   (i) Analysing the texts that emerged in the imperial contexts.
   (ii) Analysing the readings and interpretations of the texts during the colonial period.
   (iii) Understanding of the socio-political milieu of the

> readers of the texts who lived in the reality of empire, imperialism and colonialism (*Ibid.*, p. 89).

According to Sugirtharajah, "colonial reading can be summed up as informed by theories concerning the innate superiority of Western culture, the Western male as subject and the natives, heathens, women, blacks, indigenous people, as the other, needing to be controlled and subjugated" (R.S. Sugirtharajah "Biblical studies after the empire: From a colonial to a postcolonial mode of interpretation" *The Bible and Post-colonialism,* I edited by R.S. Sugirtharajah, Sheffield: Sheffield Academic Press, 1998. p. 16). He continues to state that this domineering spirit in reading practice has to be challenged. In his view what post-colonialism does is to enable us to question the totalizing tendencies of European reading practices and interpret the texts on our own terms and read them from our specific locations" (*Ibid.*, p. 16). The contextual, post-structuralist and liberative aspect of post-colonial hermeneutics is affirmed by Sugirtharajah.

## Post-Colonial Theology

Homi K. Bhabha refers to post-colonial as the form of social criticism that bears witness to the unequal and uneven process of representation by which the historical experience of the once colonized Third World come to be framed in the West, states Padmini Mongia (*Contemporary Post-colonial Theory: A Reader,* edited by Padmini Mongia, London: Arnold, 1997, p. 1).

Post-colonialism points the effects of colonialism that impacted the structures and thought, and it looks forward the deconstruction in the area of history, art, literature, philosophy and sociology. It challenges the colonial-imperialistic patterns of thought and actions and made a liberative attempt to redeem them from the distorted perspective of the West.

The colonizers (western countries) have been challenged politically, culturally and ideologically by de-colonized countries. The Western nations of power, knowledge and methodology are questioned by the colonized as they organized themselves to struggle against the dominance of the West. Though it began early, the organized form of post-colonial thought was developed as freedom of power (political independence) and freedom of thought in the nineteenth century. The people's movements are also liberative movements as they affirm the dignity, identity and rights are also the vehicles of Post-colonial ideology. The emergence of liberation theology, women theology, Black theology, *dalit* theology, tribal theology and minjung theology which are known as subaltern theologies and the effort such as contextualization/inculturation have the influence of the post-Colonial ethos.

Post-colonial theory is emerged out of the new socio-historic pressure as it is found that the new social movements around the issues such as race, gender and ethnicity have revealed the limits of older conceptions about community, individuals and nation (*Ibid.*, p. 5). Pre-colonial is interested in re-writing history in terms of the stages such as pre-colonial, colonial and post-colonial (*Ibid.*, p. 7). Post-colonial thought looks to what is 'native' and also looks forward as it challenges dominant, imperialistic world view. It is a re-reading or re-interpretation of history, methodology, theology and sources (e.g. scripture). As against the western, colonial, elitistic perspectives, the post-colonial theological and non-theological discourses argue for liberation from patriarchy, slavery and challenges gender-injustice, human right violations, and different kinds of oppressions. In post-colonial theological discourses, the indigenous or native resources are critically and creatively used as methodology is more experiential, contextual and narrative, and also there is a 'deconstruction' and decolonialisation in the whole perspectives. Post-colonialism explores the potentials of the orient. The positive elements in the eastern or Third World religions, cultures (in the form of myths, folklores, poetry, songs) and social life (historical consciousness) are explored by post-colonial ideology and theology.

According to Rey Chow, the post-colonialist affirms the resurrection of the native or challenging the dominant discourse by 'resurrecting' the victimized voice ("where have all the Natives gone?" *Contemporary Post Colonial Theory: A Reader*,. edited by Padmini Mongia, p. 129). Nationalism, sovereignty, constitutionality, self-reliance, movements towards cultural and religious roots, resistance against gender and racial prejudices and emancipatory thrust are related to post-coloniality. The marginality, Third World experience, feminity, Blackness, Asianness and Indianness, native or indigenous expressions in theology are holding the post-colonial character. The theology of the subaltern or the victimized groups are post-colonial in nature as they struggle against the imperial, colonial or oppressive powers.

According to Ruth Frankenberg and Lata Mani, for India post-colonialism means independence from Britain, birth of the nation-state, end of territorial colonialism, economic growth by the growth of indigenous capitalism, non-aligned either the first or second world ("crosscurrents, Crosstalk: Race, 'Postcoloniality' and the politics of Location", *Contemporary Post-colonial Theory,* p. 347). Post-colonialism means, for Britain the loss of most of their colonies, the appearance on British landscapes of a significant number of people from the former colonies which makes the predominantly white ethnic society into multi-racial society. It also refers to questioning Western or White dominance by the movements of resistance and the emergence of struggles for collective determination which is articulated in nationalist terms, states Ruth Frankenberg and Lata Mani (*Ibid.*, p. 348).

According to Musa W. Dube, "Post-colonial theories emanated from the rise of western empires in the eighteenth through the twentieth centuries, their scramble to divide the world among themselves, the strategies of subjugation and resistance engendered by colonialism, and the chain reactions that have been in motion ever since" ("Postcoloniality, Feminist spaces, and Religion", *Post-colonialism, Feminism and Religious Discourses,* edited by Laura E. Donaldson & Kwok Pui-lan, New York: Routledge, 2002, p. 100).

According to Dube, post-colonial feminisms display a number of recognizable strategies and concerns in their decolonizing and depatriarchalizing practices. She continues to say that post-colonial feminist operates within the past and present international oppression which continues to exert its forms of oppressions in their lives. She also states that they indicate that international oppression of the former colonies have exerted a greatest influence on colonized women (*Ibid.*, p. 115).

Dube was very conscious of the colonial forces which subjugated and silenced the women. She argues that the post colonial feminists in their reading and writing call for the decolonization of inherited colonial educational system, language, literary canons and reading methods. It is also stated that the decolonizing practices of two-thirds world feminists are accompanied by a willingness to embrace and confront indigenous religious and cultural worldview which include willingness to pronounce legitimate and adequate wherever possible, to interpret them where necessary, and to avoid the colonizing strategy of dismissing as negative all social systems of the colonized (*Ibid.*, pp. 115-116).

Dube asserts that a decolonizing feminist practices also must show how international domination renders women of former colonies politically invisible, economically impoverished, and culturally suppressed while it highlights diverse way of resistance and liberation (*Ibid.*, p. 116). Muse W. Dube insists also that post-colonial feminist strategies must confront oppressive aspects in one's own indigenous systems of gender oppressive practices such as genital mutilation and *sati*. There are rooms for re-interpreting the old and promoting good as no culture is absolutely negative or wholly pure. In these decolonizing spaces, she states, post-colonial feminist analysis wrestles with the restoration of some aspects of the indigenous cultures and reinterprets others for the empowerment of women and all people (*Ibid.*, p. 116). Post-colonial ideology questions the colonization of women's bodies especially the black, and other marginated women which began in slavery; the brutalizing sexual assault on them is criticized (M.

Shawn Copeland, "Body, representation and Black religious discourse", *Post-colonialism, Feminism & Religious Discourses*; p. 182). The discrimination in the name of gender or race is questioned by post-colonialism.

According to R.S. Sugirtharajah, the Western modes of scientific thinking whether it is liberal, rational or positivist only can enslave us, so we have to be freed from them. The indigenous or native expressions and thought patterns are to be upheld (*The Bible and the Third World*, Cambridge: Cambridge University Press, 2001, p. 176). The central task of post-colonial biblical interpretation is described as recovery, reoccupation and reinscription of one's culture which has been degraded and affected from the colonial narratives and from mainstream Biblical scholarship, states Sugirtharajah (*Ibid.*, p. 177). According to him, "Vernacular hermeneutics tries to erase the painful memory of this degradation and effacement, and to make a fresh start by returning to one's roots. Impelled by a variety of cultural and political forces, it is an attempt to go 'home'. It is a call to self-awareness, aimed at creating an awakening among people to their indigenous literary, cultural and religious heritage" (*Ibid.*, p. 177). Vernacular is understood as nativism, cultural nationalism, indigenous, struggle for the historical and political presences of groups suppressed or marginalized by colonization and modernization, an assertion and selfhood and self-respect instead of slavish conformity to received ideas, valuing the indigenous resources and deep distrust of the centralizing tendencies of Euro-American critical theories. (*Ibid.*, p. 177).

The post-colonial intertexual reading is found in the biblical interpretation. According to Sugirtharajah, the post-colonial interpretation has the vocation to de-ideologizing dominant interpretation and the distrust of the totalizing, tendencies (*Ibid.*, p. 224). Sugitharajah states again, post-colonial theory offers a space for the once colonized. It is an interpretative act of the descendants of those once subjected. In effect, it means a resurrection of the marginal, the indigene and subaltern" (*Ibid.*, p. 250).

The task of the post-colonial criticism, according to Sugirtharajah, is to engage in reconstructive reading of Biblical texts. In his words, 'postcolonial reading will reread Biblical texts from the perspective of postcolonial concerns such as liberation struggles of the past and present; it will be sensitive to subaltern and feminine elements embedded in texts' (*Ibid.*, p. 252).

Post-colonial theology is narrative, liberative, nativistic and people-oriented. It upholds the struggle of the oppressed and goes against the elites or dominant class and the colonizers. There is a re-understanding of theology as post-colonial theology challenges the Western thinking and methodology which is more individualistic, abstract capital intensive and imperialistic. Post-colonial theology is concerned of the marginalized or subaltern such as poor, women, blacks, *dalits* and tribes. It re-reads the scripture in the light of the aspirations of the victimized and also give importance to the indigenous resources. It does value what is native.

The post-colonial theology is also having the elements of post-structuralism and post-modernism. The aspects such as orientalism, nationalism, indigeneity, and contextuality play vital roles in post-colonial theology. It also deconstructs the traditional, dominant and western forms of ideology and theology. Post-colonial theology challenges the authoritarian structures and it sides the oppressed or marginated. The subaltern experience and their consciousness is also very crucial in post-colonial theology. Post-colonial theology is also liberative. It challenges patriarchy, caste hierarchy, racial discrimination and hegemony. The empowerment of *dalits*, tribes, victimized women, blacks and other suffering humanity is an essential concern of post-colonial theology.

## Post-Colonial Ethics

Post-colonialism challenges the colonialism and it resists the impositions and importation of any value system from the West or from the dominant groups. Neo-colonialism or globalization is the new form of colonization taking place all over the world. The powerless erstwhile colonized countries are badly affected by globalization. Globalization is an imposition of the culture, economic and political policies of the hegemonic forces (Western Countries) over the Third World.

Following are the characteristic of post-colonial ethics:

### *(1) Post-colonial Ethics is Anti-hegemonic*

It is not compromising with the powerful or the dominant forces. It is concerned of the issues of the colonized. As we see in post-modernism, it is against the totalizing of the hegemonic forces and their structures. So it is post-structural in nature. The values of the dominant powers and the imposition of their ideologies are rejected by post-colonialism. It questions the oppressive and exploitative elements.

### *(2) Post-colonial Ethics is Contextual*

Post-colonialism affirms the contextuality. The experience of the decolonized or the indigenous people are very significant for post-colonialism. The particular context, the pluralism, the persons and people are considered in contextual ethics. The struggles of the people of the third world and their socio-economic realities and the stark reality of poverty are responded in post-colonial ethics. Post-colonial ethics is praxis-oriented.

### *(3) Post-colonial Ethics is Liberative*

Post-colonial ethics looks for deconstruction as we see in post-modernism. It challenges existing structures of domination (Western and Eastern) and look forward a radical restructuring of the society. Spivak was pointing the disregard towards the subaltern. Their identity and crisis are to be taken into account when we deal with post-colonial ethics. The victimized groups need empowerment and liberation. They include *dalits*, tribes, transgenders, blacks, other indigenous groups and victimized women. Post-colonial ethics is an ethics of the poor, powerless and victimized. It challenges the oppressing and exploitative structures. It is a decolonizing ethics.

The issue of land, nationalism, poverty, women, *dalits*, tribes, blacks and other marginalized groups and the struggle for equal distribution of resources and empowerment are major concerns in post-colonial theology and ethics. Post-colonial ethics is not rooted in what is classical, western or dominant, but radical as it is indigenous, people-oriented and anti-hegemonic.

## Post-colonialism and Indian Scenario

According to Jyotirmaya Tripathy (IIT, Madras) Post-colonialism should not be reduced to a literary theory, but has to be understood as a lived experience and a political condition. It also has to transcend the conventional indictment of Eurocentrism, Jyotirmaya states (from the abstract of the paper 'How Post-colonial is post-colonial India? http://ocs.sfu.ca/ac/a/s/viewpaper,php?Id215/print2 accessed on 11/09/2013). Jyotirmaya observes that during the independence movements, Arya Samajists believed British rule was much less harmful than Islamic regimes. Indian freedom struggle spearheaded by Gandhiji and Nehru was understood as an elite discourse to which leaders of Hindu revivalism did not subscribe (*Ibid.,* p. 1). Jyotirmaya also points out that colonialism was not with the British rule, but with the Islamic invasion in 10th century and continued through Delhi sultanate to Mughal empire. In the words of Jyotirmaya, "when Britishers colonized India, they were colonizing an already colonized land, and some sections of Indians were celebrating freedom from Mughal rule" (*Ibid.*, p. 1). Jyotirmaya again states, "Given this India is both a settler and invaded post-colonial society. If it is the former, the authentic post-colonial voice is that of a Hindu, if it is the latter, it is the secular voice of India" (*Ibid.,* p. 1).

Jyotirmaya Tripathy's observations about post-colonialism from the Hindu revivalists' point of view is worthy to ponder about. The Islamic invasion and their settlement is totally different from the colonial rule of the British. The Islamic and non-islamic communities have undergone the struggle under British colonial power and other European powers who have exploited our valuable resources and sent them to their country.

It is interesting to look at the question of Reshmi R. Dasgupta, 'Is bread and butter pudding Indian or British'? In her article 'Living in Post-colonial India: embracing British culture' (http:/ articles economitimes.indiatemes.com/2012-05-08-accessed on 11/9/2013. p 1). It is true that we are regulated by British culture though we live in a post-colonial era. The baked food and bakery are colonial 'contribution'. People are also after the taste of Kentuky Fried Chicken which is foreign. We are Indians, but are after foreign food and other materials. We are after foreign food and other foreign items than the indigenous food and materials.

We are trying to adopt the food habits and life-style of the European countries. There is also a fascination for the 'foreign'. A change in attitude and life style in essential to overcome the colonial spirit. It is very important to value our traditions, the potentials, history and philosophy, then only we can overcome the spirit of colonialism.

## The Indian Christian Theology as Post-colonial

It is important to ask the question can the subalterns speak which was raised by Gayatri Spivak. There can be many phases to Indian christian theology. In the Brahminic-Advaitic Phase, there are thinkers such as Raja Rammohun Roy, Keshub Chander Sen, Brahma Badhav Upadhyay, Goreh, Pierre Johanns, K.M. Banerjea, Sister Vandana, Dhanji Bhai Fakirbhai, Manilal Parekh. In the Bhakti phase there are thinkers like P. Chenchiah, Venkal Chakkarai, A.J. Appasamy and Śadhu Sundersingh. In the dialogical and Inter-religious phase there are theologians like Farquhar, Hogg, Monchanin, Amalorpavadas, Abhishiktanda, P.D. Devanandan, Raymond Panikkar, and S.J. Samartha. The subaltern-liberative phase has figures and theologies like Sebastian

Kappen, M.M. Thomas, K.C. Abraham, Paulose Mar Paulose, Nirmal Minz, Arvind Nirmal, K. Thanzuava, Abraham Ayrookuzhiel, M.E. Prabhakar, V. Devasahayan, Gabriele Dietrich, Prasannakumari, R.L. Hnuni, Lalrinwami Ralte, Monica Melanchthon, Evangeline-Rajkumar and Aruna Gnanadason (Liberation theology, Feminist theology, Dalit theology and tribal/Adivasi theology).

The orthodox phase has theologians like Pulos Mar Gregorios, V.C. Samuel, Geevarghese Mar Osthathios and Dr. K.M. George. There is also Evangelical phase of theology (Sundersingh, Paul Sudhakar, Vinay Samuel and Sunand Sumithra), and pentecostal-charismatic phase of theology, so also the eco-theology.

Indian Christian theology is now becoming indigenous, political and contextual in nature. The early phase of Indian Christian theology was highly Advaitic, abstract and Brahminical. It was also elitistic, as the issues of the subalterns and the victimized or oppressed were not considered. Though it was an effort to make an indigenized theology as to move away from the western theologies, it was keeping silent to the voice of the subalterns. The early Indian Christian theology was the theology of the dominant and it was based on the philosophical system (*Advaita*, *dvaita* or *visistadvaita*) of the dominant caste.

It is to be noticed that the consiousness of the *dalits*, tribes/*Adivasis*, the women or the poor are not taken into consideration in the early Indian Christian theology. So it was a change from Western elitistic theology to Indian elitistic theology. The present phase of Indian Christian theology, however, gives utmost importance to the questions and aspirations of the subalterns. A real and adequate post-colonial theology in India cannot surpass the voices, visions and resources of the poor and marginalized. The issues of the *dalit* and tribal women are important over here. It is also so happened that Indian feminist theology focused on the voice of the elite Indian women. Now, the concerns of Subaltern women are taken up. The alienation and oppression against the transgenders is another significant issue. They are also looking forward their emancipation and empowerment. The identity, dignity and rights of the subalterns are to be recognized in order to formulate an appropriate post-colonial theology in the Indian context. It is important to maintain the characteristics such as deconstruction or delegitimization, spirit of decolonizing, indigeneity or contextuality and liberation. The resources of the subalterns are to be used in formulating the post-colonial theology in the Indian context.

The subalterns are for a redemption or liberation from the dehumanization. The emancipation or empowerment is what they look for. They are for their resources which are cultural and social. They also challenge the cultural economic and political oppressions of the neo-colonial forces. The tribes of Niyamgiri (Odisha) are questioning the Bauxites mining which will endanger the life of the people and their habitat, so also resources. Narmada valley struggle and the struggles in Nandigram, the famous chipko movement and the Chengara (Kerala) are the example of the emergence of the subalterns for their identity, dignity and rights.

The subaltern (*dalits*, tribes, victimized women, transgenders, the poor and other marginalized groups) hermaneutics and theology have to consider spheres or phases of experience. First sphere is the experience of the oppressed past. Second sphere is the present experience of indignity, inhumanity and the liberative struggle for empowerment, and the third sphere is the vision of future where there is a state of dignity, rights, identity, empowerment or liberation. Here there should be also a focus on the continuing struggle to maintain their status against the oppressive forces. It should be kept in mind that the subalterns had a distant past where they had the equal status and dignity.

## Post-Colonialism and Pentecostalism

Pentecostalism is the ideology of a movement of pentecostals. It is a movement of protest and revival of a group of people who belonged to different religions, races, castes and social status. They have a common identity as pentecostals, but there are different identities geographically and ethnically.

Pentecostals uphold holiness, unity, fellowship (koinonia) and renewal or transformation. In the West, there are white and black roots for pentecostalism. The white pentecostal movement was spearheaded by Charles Parham (USA) and the black roots which is stronger than the white pentecostal movement was led by William Joseph Seymour, an American black. In India, there are *dalit* and tribal pentecostals as there are elite or dominant pentecostals.

Pentecostalism is post-colonial in nature as it is anti-pyramidal and deconstructive. It challenges the authoritarian structures which are promoted by religions, society and mainline churches. It is anti-authoritarian, and anti-hierarchical. It is a people-centred movement and liberative. Most of the pentecostal churches give more importance to the indignity. The contextual elements from the society and culture are critically adapted. Simple church structure, local dress codes and free-church model of worship (spontaneous worship, not liturgical) and narrative preaching are some of the examples for this. Pentecostalism was a protest movement as it challenges the structures of domination which has a colonial spirit. So it has an aspect of decolonizing.

The pentecostal movement was a protest and liberative movement as it was not only a challenge to mainline churches, but also a challenge to social structures which dehumanize people. The poor, blacks, *dalits*, the tribes, the slaves and the down-trodden men and women who can be called subalterns looking for a mobility, empowerment and emancipation from the clutches of dominant forces of oppression, are finding identity in pentecostal movement. The Subalterns have a continuing struggle in pentecostal movement as some dominant forces, as against its original ideology, deny their active participation, rights leadership, and identity and dignity. To an extent, the colonial forces of disintegration, discrimination and inequality at work in certain pentecostal groups. Here it is important to recognize the liberating voice of the Subalterns.

It is also to be noted that there are churches of the dominant pentecostals, and churches for the Subaltern pentecostals. The black pentecostal churches and *dalit* pentecostal churches are to be mentioned here. The spontaneous form of churches in the name of ethnic diversity is not an issue, but the deliberate discriminative attempt to disintegrate the subalterns is a serious ideological, theological and existential problem. In this regard, the post-colonial ideology is a great support to the empowerment of the subaltern pentecostals. God is not for degradation, inequality and prejudice (Gen 1:27, 28; Gal 3:28; Acts 10). God is pro-subaltern (pro-poor, pro-black, pro-*dalit*, pro-tribes, and pro-victimized women).

Though there is the issue of subalterns among pentecostals, pentecostal movement is on the whole is having the temper and character of post-colonialism. Pentecostal movement is inclusive as it is open to people from different ethnic groups and social status. It is transformative and liberative as people who undergoes different crises and those who are oppressed by the dominant castes and classes are accommodated. The worship, singing, preaching, the structure of the church, the doctrines and practices are very contextual in nature, so they uphold the spirit of post-colonialism. Most of the pentecostal churches are indigenous in character, so they are redeemed from the clutches of Eurocentrism and the domineering spirit.

## Concluding Remarks

Colonialism follows a exclusivistic and disintegrative type of ideology which is dehumanizing and oppressive. The post-colonial ideology is inclusive, integrating and liberating. Post-colonialism affirms pluralism and indigeneity. The Subaltern identity or identities such as *dalits*, tribes, blacks, women (non-elite women), transgenders and the poor and their struggles are considered seriously in post-colonialism. Post-colonial philosophical framework is concrete contextual and experiential rather than abstract and elitistic. What is colonized has to be decolonized and this process has to take place in the area of culture including languages, social life, perspectives, the various studies including philosophy and social sciences. The oppressive and dehumanizing attitude to the 'other' has to be questioned.

# 2
# Traditional, Modern and the Question of Development

By the coming of enlightenment, there is a conflict between traditional and modernity. It is always made the people to think that what is traditional is bad and what is modern is good and best. The modern understanding of development is also very much promoted by those tho would like to live in comfort Zones.

## What is Traditional?

The new generation people, sometimes, do not understand what is traditional. They are not familiar with the traditional setting. Those who live in rural areas may have some idea about what is traditional. The urbal context has thoroughly wiped out what is traditional. Traditional is what is historically found in the local context and the similar contexts. The value system, life style, eating habits, cooking patterns, the dress codes, the educational system and the health care are indigenous or native in nature in the traditional setting.

The Westerners and the eastern elites are trying to undermine and uproot the traditional setting by insisting that their ways of thinking and doing are better than what is existing in the context. It is an imposition of what is western on the local indigenous people. Traditional religious experiences, philosophical insights, medicines and wisdom are being challenged and considered as good for nothing by the West. Now certain changes are taking place in the attitudes as Indian philosophical thoughts, religious views and medical care (e.g. Ayurveda) are considered as valuable by the Westerners. Western thinkers have now found Indian religious and cultural resources as valuable, as they quote from *Bhagavad Gita*, *Upanishads* and Budhist and Jainist traditions.

The Indian and Western elites have an aversion towards what is traditional. They degrade Indian culture and religion. The Westerners especially colonizers found Indian traditional setting as inferior and sub-standard. They fail to understand what is good in traditional and to correct or modify what is not useful. They had, instead, followed a rejectionist attitude towards what is traditional.

## What is Modern?

Modern is the contribution of enlightenment in the form of Science and technology. Indian way of education is eradicated and Western education system is introduced. Instead of Indian medicines, the allopathic is introduced. In the name of modern, the Western elements are trusted upon us. The Western music, dance, habits, food and values are found everywhere in our context. Our vernacular is slowly wiped out, whereas English is introduced as the medium of instruction. Instead of Hindi, English became our link-language. Our Kitchen is electrified (e.g. microwave and induction cooker) and also liquefied petroleum gas is used as fuel than the traditional firewood. Most of the houses have no chimneys to use firewood.

The industrialization has also contributed much to modernization. The world is highly mechanized. The products are important than human beings. The consumerism, profiteering and market economy or globalization are the regulating factors of the economic context. The ecological disaster is mainly the contribution of industrialization. The emission of toxic materials (chloro-fluoro oxides, carbon dioxide, sulphur dioxide and carbon mono-oxide) and the chemical and nuclear wastes are contributing to different pollutions (air, water and soil), damaged one the ozone layer and the depletion of natural resources like water, minerals, and fossil fuels.

The wetlands are lost, the bio-diversity is adversely affected and the whole of creation is facing threat to the survival. The modern concept of development is neither eco-friendly nor people-friendly. The word development becomes the most misused term as it is used to make Comfort Zone for the powerful and rich at the expense of poor. Poor are chased away from their habit at in the name of development such as Nuclear plants, hydro-electric projects (dams) and Special Economic Zones. Poor are evacuated from their habitat for the comfort of the rich, which is called as 'development' by scientists, technocrafts, bureaucrats, and industrialist and the government. This is certainly a distortion.

## What is Colonial?

Colonialism and imperialism are the attitudes of human beings to subjugate others. It develops inhuman minds and are implemented in intellectual, social, economical, religious and political realms. Colonial and imperial interests are found in Aryans and other Europeans. The Spaniards, Portuguese, Dutch, French and the Britishers were the main colonializers. They were interested in land, political power and the tapping of recources. They used 'divide and rule' policy over the natives and gained political and economic power. They used oppressive and exploitative methods to subjugate the natives.

The colonizers have almost wiped out the Maoris, Amerindians and Red Indians in an uncivilized manner. They have conquered many islands, Asia, Africa and Latin America. The western colonial powers have made roads, railway tracks and seaports for transporting the exploits to their countries which is misunderstood by natives as development. Certainly, it is for the development of the West. The native medicine, wisdom, for the system of rule, communal life, life style and food habits are wiped out by the West and introduced their own as the best. It is observed that the colonial powers have introduced bakeries and colonized the people through the taste of the baking food. The baking and fried food which is tasty, but through that also introduced the cardiac diseases.

Now the colonialism is almost gone, but the neo-colonialism is at its heights. We are made dependent on the Westerners and their multinational corporations or Transnational Corporations. They found also native collaborators to support them, so that they can easily implement their policies and sell their products. They appear as messiahs, but wolves in the guise of sheep. In Somalia, the Westerners appears as 'Saviours' to help the sheep from the diseases. At first, they freely provided medicine, then they taxed for medicine. At last they said that they will provide meat by that they destroyed the sheep-rearing which was a major traditional employment for many Somalians. They provided the least quality meat in cheap rate to destroy their trade. The local people are later on left to poverty and unemployment. The colonial and neo-colonial elements are found within a country as they sell, by crooked means, the resources (coal, iron ore, minerals etc.) to native and foreign mafia groups without considering the people's interests. No one is found accountable and answerable to people. so the question is asked, 'who is the original owner of the resources?' and 'who has the right to sell all there resources?'

## What is Development?

Development is understood by many people as imitating the patterns of the West. It is a misunderstanding. The things that West have introduced for their comfort are understood as what is 'developed'. The modern cooking wares, the computer, Television and other electric instruments are considered as part of modern development. The old cooking system is gone and heavily depending on liquefied petroleum Gas. We come to a position that we cannot live without electricity and cooking gas.

The population is growing so also the migration of the rural people to the urban areas. The consumption of food is more and also the use of electricity. But we are fall short of the demand as there is a severe power or energy crisis. We are moved to a 'developed' stage from where we cannot come down. Then, the price of these things are also going up, and common people cannot afford it. The rich are not worried about the price-hike, they are only worried about the availability of these.

In the name of 'modern' and 'development' certain things are trusted upon the people and later on lead the people to troubled waters by taxing much. The privatization and liberalization are the forms of neo-colonial policies which eliminate the government control and reduces the subsidies. The dictate of World Bank, IMF and Asian Development Bank do control our economic and political system. As Gunther Grass has opined the Indian bureaucrats are stout as they are corrupt. They are 'developing' so much, but the poor and powerless are starving. A group of people in the upper ladder of the hierarchy are enjoying all privileges and benefits and 'developing' but those who are in the lower ladder are struggling for shelter, clothing, food, health-care, employment and education.

Those who are earning more movers should render some amount to the welfare and the development of the poor. Their empowerment is much needed in our context today. The luxury of the rich and their pompous life is not what is development, but the empowerment of the rural poor, the *dalits*, tribes, the slum-dwellers and the urban poor. In India, a large number of people undergo the struggle for survival and small number of people enjoy all privileges. The rich accumulate and monopolize the income generating resources and the poor have no access to them.

When India's Planning Commission has set Rs. 28 as a norm for poverty-line (if anybody is getting more than Rs. 28 per day, they are above poverty-line), a cartoon came in a national daily showing the picture of a family which dwells in the street. A car was stopped before them and extended some money, but they rejected it telling that they have already received Rs. 28. It means that looking at the troubles of being a person belonging to APL (Above Poverty Line), he denied the help. This exposes the paradoxical life of an Indian. No one asked the real question of whether one can survive with Rs. 28 per day. These norms are set for the powerless, and not for the rich and powerful.

The mafia groups have acquired the land and they decide the price or value of the land. By unjust means they get the land and make flats and villas and make a big Real Estate business. The most developing industry in India is Real Estate business. It marginalizes powerless people and stands for the development of the rich and the powerful. It is quite important to note that many rich invest their money in hotel business, land and construction of flats and villas, health-care (e.g. private hospitals) and create a "demand" for their survival. No space is available, so we have to depend the Real Estate people. The Real Estate people are also behind the private hospitals, where big amount of money is charged for treatment. Appealing and unrealistic advertisements are made to attract the patients by these firms.

What we need is a sustainable development. The development has to consider the ecological concerns. The total development of the poor should have the priority. Their shelter, food, employment, education and health-care should be the central concern of development. Development should be people-friendly, integral or holistic and eco-friendly. The poor, *dalits*, tribes, differently abled, victimized women and children undergo serious struggles and they are to be considered in development. Justice and human rights play a vital role in the issue of development. The food, security, welfare and equitable distribution of resources are also crucial in the search for holistic development.

The capitalistic structures are promoting a 'trickle down theory' which argues that when a group economically grow, others will also automatically grow along with them. This is a false theory. Unless everyone has the access to income-generating resources, the poor cannot economically grow. No development efforts will succeed unless the development of the poor and marginalized is achieved. In the present economic system, the rich and powerful can obtain more benefits, and the poor are neglected. It is set for the benefit and profit of the powerful than the poor. The Indian government and its development programmes and also the rich and the powerful should find an answer for the question: 'how long it will take to have a realistic development and empowerment/emancipation of the marginalized of India? India has claimed a growth in science and technology. We take pride in our missiles and satellites, but it is also a fact that the condition of the poor is not improved, and many are finding refuge in streets and slums.

## What is the Reality?

It is very important to look into the stark reality of suffering millions. Millions of people are refugees because of war, disasters and internal political crisis. Now the world population is 700 crores, and by 2050, the population will become 900 crore. According to World Hunger Report, 1/7 of the population of the world is in extreme hunger. Because of the population growth, every year we have to find food for eight crore new people. In India more than 35 per cent of the population live in extreme food insecurity [*Malayala Manorama* (daily newspaper) 15th October, 2012, p. 4].

While there is the so called development, there is also the 'development' of slums. It shows the increasing process of marginalization. The rich and powerful enjoy the effect of 'development' and the poor and powerless are pushed to the periphery. It is a paradoxical situation. Slums are the cancer of our society which are at the increase. In Western countries, there are people living with first, second and third estate status, and a big number of people live in ghettoes. Almost 25 per cent of Indian urban population are slum-dwellers. Dr. Godwin Shiri states that the increasing number of slums in which millions live a sub-human life reveals a deep-rooted system of malady, raising doubts about the very effectiveness of the development policies pursued by our country (*Our Slums: Mirror a systemic malady*, Bangalore: ATC, 1999, p. 1).

The data shows that the conditions of the suffering ones is pathetic. 80 per cent of the world resources are availed by 20 per cent of the rich and powerful. According to a UN report, around 25,000 children die out of hunger everyday, and out of 202 crore children 100 crore live in poverty. It is estimated that around 25 per cent of the children are malnourished. In India, 70 per cent of the people earn only Rs. 20 to 50 per day.

In India, more than 60 per cent of the people do not have proper sanitation facilities. Around 95 per cent of the people of India do not have access to clean drinking water. According to a study, the population of the elderly in India is expected to increase to 173 million by 2026, and nearly three out of five single older women are very poor. Out of 90 million elderly persons of India, 30 million are living alone and 90 per cent of them work for their livelihood [Aarti Dhar, "Concerns over an aging India", *The Hindu* (October 7, 2012), p. 13]. Illiterary, poverties, malnutrition and unemployment are the plights of our country. Many children do not go to school or drop at an early stage as there is no economic support. Children are also seeking employment to support their homes, so child labour is at the increase in Indian situation.

In many *dalit* and tribal pockets there is no school or there is schools without inadequate facilities. The government schools are being closed down and the private schools and colleges are coming up. They are having only monetary interest. There are investors behind these private educational institutions (e.g. schools, colleges including engineering and medical colleges) who act like falcons (falconry) to oppress the people, especially the poor, to make money. The poor cannot withstand the exploitative situation.

The condition of the poor is miserable as many do not have land or shelter, so they find refuge near railway tracks, pavements and streets. The *dalits*, tribes and the victimized women are finding problem with their identity, dignity and rights. They live in oppressed and dehumanized situation. Domestic and societal violence against women is common in our context. The *dalits* and tribes are evacuated forcefully from their habitat, as many of them do not have title deeds, though they are the original inhabitants of the land. Many original inhabitants of this country are now not considered as the citizens of this country, which is a paradox.

What is the destiny of the poor and powerless? They live in a deserted, scattered and crushed condition. The worst victims of food, water, diseases, and ecological problems are the poor. Many poor live with or without a square meal. Many poor are landless labourers and bond-slaves. They are also debtors to their land owners. There are girls and women who become sex-workers because of extreme poverty. The social inequality is contributed by caste system, lack of economic stability and unjust political policies. The public distribution system is also faulty, as many poor cannot get privileges as they have no ration cards. They have no ration card as they have no land of their own or shelter (house). The Indian soil is for everyone who is born in this country or who became a citizen of this country, and no one is supposed to suppress or manipate another. The powerful have no right to subjugate and exploit the powerless.

## A Critical Response and Reflection

What is the kind of community and development we need? What we look forward is a just social order, where everyone will have a meaningful survival based on peace and justice which includes the right to food, shelter, education, employment, health care, security and freedom.

It is important to have a critical look at development. It is always important to affirm what is good and challenge what is evil. There are good elements in tradition, modernity and development. There are also negative elements which are to be rejected. What is humane and just is important over here.

Uprooting and destroying what is valuable and good for the people is sin. It is also a sin, if we misguide the people with selfish interests in order to impose our products and ideas. This is very much happening in the global market.

Globalization is the neo-colonialism and it promotes market economy. It is a neo-liberal policy which revolves around the liberal or capitalistic economic policy of Adam Smith which argues for a free and self-regulating market or economic affair. The intervention of state is disallowed in his law of economics. Discussing the economic policy of Adam Smith, Jacob Prasad states, "the laws of economics, he believed, lead to the prosperity of all nations provided that one allows them to work without outside intervention, i.e. intervention by the state. Each strives for riches and through absolute competition the 'selfish agents in the market hold one another in check and advance developments in a way which is favourable for all' (Biblical perspectives on a fair and just economic order", *Jeevadhara* [Vol. XLI, No. 242 (March 2011), p. 100]. He continues to say that, "However, history has shown that the application of this economistic faith did not lead to the prosperity of all, and of all nations. Within the nations, the masses became improverished" (*Ibid.*, p. 100). Adam Smith has promoted a capitalist system, where the powerful can achieve their goal of accumulating wealth.

The welfare state concept or welfarism is proposed by John Maynard Kaynes. He does not believe in the autonomous self-regulation of the market, but argues for the conscious political direction, states Jacob Prasad, by using the criteria such as justice and peace (*Ibid.*, p. 101). Amartya Sen also supports the welfare economics where he argues for the 'Safety net' to support the poor. Welfarism is also not a very radical or liberative process. It only creates some supportive systems to the poor.

The major trend in economics is the globalization. It creates competition in the field of economics. It is a neo-colonial system by which powerful can obtain a large profit by promoting a consumeristic ideology. It aims at creating a market economy as it is capital-intensive. The multi-national companies control the market as they impose their products. It takes every effort to destroy the local products. The patent laws, the terminated seed, and the heavy taxation are the example of the impositions. The New Economic Policy and Structural Adjustment Programme are in support of globalization. The Global investors, either directly enter into the Third World market or in collaboration with the local business lobbies. The only intention they have is to exploit the local resources and make maximum profit by selling their products. It is a falconry.

The World Bank, the International Monetary Fund, the Asian Development Bank and similar funding agencies have also paid money for Third World countries as loans in order to develop the infrastructure. When these countries are not able to pay the interests, they advise them to increase the rate of electricity, water and to cut off the subsidy on ration, domestic gas and fertilizer. They also suggest the increase of tax. These can make the life of the people, especially the poor, miserable.

Morality is an important factor for the adequate economies and development. According to P.V. Shenoi, "In the economic world, morality ideally stands for good faith, full value of money, transparency, goodwill and freedom from exploitation (*Market and Morality,* Bangalore: Ecumenical Christian Centre, 2002, p. 6). What we need is a sustainable development which includes poverty alleviation, eco-friendly industrial and agricultural development, empowerment of subalterns, employment generation, equitable distribution of resources for everyone's welfare, a proper and reasonable distributive system and the infrastructure—roads, health and sanitation, education, security, power and transport. Measure are to be taken to uphold the identity, dignity and rights of everyone, especially the powerless. An eco-friendly and people-friendly development will only become successful.

Bible is for the sustainable development of everyone, especially the powerless (Lev. 25). The Jubilee is a restoring principle and covenant is a liberating principle which look forward the total welfare and sustainable development of the people. The liberative or empowering principles are found also in the Exodus-event, the second Exodus and also in the teaching of prophets and Jesus. The oppressive structure of corruption and exploitation which stood against the welfare of the poor and worked for a feudal economic system was challenged by prophets (1 kgs, 21; Am. 4:1-2; Am 5:10-13). The rich were living at the expense of the poor and they sought their own growth and development. They had an imperial or colonial spirit to accumulate wealth for themselves. The prophets have challenged that inhuman attitude.

Jesus' teaching was based on the Kingdom of God. The Nazareth manifesto (Lk 4:16-21) stands for the total welfare and development or liberation of the poor and marginalized. Kingdom of God is rooted in peace and justice. The Kingdom community is the focus of Jesus where everyone should have equity, rights and dignity. Jesus was for the humanizing of the subalterns. He did challenge the powerful for their exploitative nature (Lk 12:13-21, Lk 17:19-31; Lk 19:1-10). He was also aware of the exploitative relationship of economics, politics and religion which make the life of the common people difficult. This is very evident in Jesus' attack on the business that was going on in the temple. Jesus was concerned of the restoration and emancipation or empowerment of the poor, sick and victimized groups. Jesus did radically question the oppressive factors that hinder the total development and empowerment of the people, especially the subalterns.

The people-friendly and eco-friendly development is possible as the liberative spirit of religions and cultures are to be explored. Aloysius Pieris, the Srilankan Theologian, observes the positive poles and negative poles in religion. Positive pole, for him, is liberative. This can be also applied to culture and tradition. M.M. Thomas stated that Jesus affirms and humanizing elements found in socio-political structures and culture, and condemns the inhuman elements (*Some Theological Dialogues*, Bangalore: CISRS, 1977. pp. 70 ff). He also advocated a 'spirituality of combat'. He also argues for right to bread, right to equality and self-determination. Fr. Sebastian Kappen stood for a counter-culture or liberative spirit which is found in Christianity, Budhism, Jainism, Bhakti movements and in Marxism.

What we should seek is not 'trickle down effect', but the total or holistic and sustainable development of the people. Medha Patkar challenges the investor-driven model of development and monopolisation of resources as she states, "the investor-driven development model deprives thousands of people the resources by which they base their livelihood" (*The Hindu,* November 18, 2012, p. 4).

## Concluding Remarks

The tradition and modernity have certain positive poles or liberative spirit, so also very rigid and evil elements. The unrealistic and irrelevant kinds of principles and perspectives are to be challenged. A critical and creative look into our tradition, culture, religious and ideologies is essential to identify the oppressive and colonial factors and to respond to them.

Development concepts are varied in forms as they have different intentions. Investors are always having the mind of eagles or wolves, as they try to exploit and to accumulate wealth for themselves.

The globalized market economy is capital intensive and is free market economy. It is a *laissez faire* economy. It is not people-friendly or eco-friendly. The poor are not taken care in that view of development. What we need is a alternative, poor-friendly and eco-friendly development. The empowerment of poor, *dalits*, tribes, children, women and the mentally and physically challenged are to be highly regarded. The hindrances such as self-interested politics, corruption and selfish economic interest should go in order to achieve the people-friendly development.

# 3

# Response to Violence Against Dalits and Tribes

This is an attempt to deal with the violence against *dalits* and tribes, who are the indigenous people of India. They are the most victimized groups as they are exploited and oppressed by several ways. Violence is used against them by the dominant castes and class groups and also the government machinery. So, it is important to identify with the causes of these marginalized people and to respond to their issues. It provides only some general ideas about the condition of *dalits* and tribes and also a response to them.

## A. Dalit Issues and Responses

The *dalits* confront several crucial issues in the Indian context. They face several forms of violence, which is described in the following paragraphs:

### *1. Caste System*

Caste system is a hierarchical structure of discrimination developed by Brahmainic system. It is an Aryan crude method to dehumanize the Dravidians. The English word 'caste' is derived from the Spanish/Portughese word 'casta' which means race, breed or lineage. According to M.N. Srinivas, caste system is a hereditary endogamous and localized group having a traditional occupation and a definite position in the hierarchy of caste. There are different theories behind the origin of caste system. The theories are as follows:

### *(a) Varna Theory*

Caste was developed on the basis of colour in the Vedic period. There was a difference between Arya and Anarya. Brahmin, Kshatrya and Vaisya belonged to Aryavarna. Sudra and panchamas belonged to the Anarya or Dasavarna. This theory insists the Varnashrama Dharma or caste duty. The Hindu scriptures subscribe the caste system by saying that Brahmins, Kshatryas, Vaisyas and Sudras come out of Brahman's mouth/head, hands, thighs and feet respectively.

### *(b) Priestly Theory*

According to this theory caste system is the creation of the priestly class in order to assert their superiority over others.

### *(c) Functional Theory/Occupational Theory*

The differences in occupations have resulted in the caste system. The people who do similar jobs grouped together and formed as guilds and which give form to caste system.

### *(d) Ritual Theory*

The purity consciousness in rituals and family meals exclude others and this had led to the development of caste system. The theories have their own problems. The main question is how the pollution has occurred in caste system. There was a definite attempt by some selfish groups to undermine the dignity and identity of other groups. It is done by either forcing them to do menial jobs, or by considering them as inferior on the basis of colour or by regarding them as impure because of colour and the occupation. The caste becomes an essential part of Hindu religious tradition. The Aryans claimed that they are the dominant race and subjugate others by the use of force or by misuse of religion. It is interesting to note that Dr. S. Radhakrishnan and Gandhiji equated caste system with class system. They failed to see the dehumanizing elements in caste system. The pollution and discrimination associated to caste system are evils. Jainism and Buddhism protested the caste system. Dr. B.R. Ambedkar and Jyotirao Phule were strongly challenging the evils of caste system. Caste system is like apartheid. There is a strong element of untouchability in it. Education, employment, access to income generating resources, increasing participation in the socio-political life and furnishing their rights can be the means to help them to come out of their present status of discrimination and indignity. The caste identity should be realized only as a community identity and not as means to underestimate a group of people in the name of birth, colour or occupation. The main problem with caste system is that a person is born with indignity which is a serious discrimination.

Though the Christian principle is not supporting the caste system, the dominant groups try to enslave others and oppress them. The dominate groups control the Church for accomplishing their interests. The *dalits* are used by the Church and society for their selfish interests and as vote banks. It is interesting to note that there were separate churches and cemeteries built in certain places for the *dalits* to affirm the completion of discrimination.

According to Gandhiji, untouchability is a crime against God and man. Bible states that all human beings are created with equal dignity and no one is to be discriminated (Gen 1:27, 28). Jesus regarded highly the dignity and status of all so called outcastes like samaritans, lepers, diseased, non-jews and the poor. He loved them and healed them. Apostle Paul also holds a vision that transcends the disparities (Gal 3:28). The Christian community should be an agent of transformation in the society to challenge what is evil. It should also act as models by which others could also follow the path. It is important to know that man is God's creation and he should not be discriminated by any reason.

## 2. Dalit Population

There are 13.82 crore of people belonging to scheduled castes in the country. This constitutes 16.48 per cent of the country's total population. The states of UP, West Bengal, Bihar and Andhra Pradesh account more than 50 per cent of the scheduled caste population (*Malayala Manorama Year book 2010*, p. 580). The literacy rate of *dalits* is around 37 per cent, compared to the national average of 52 per cent. The *dalits* in Kerala constitute 9.81 per cent (31,24,600). The main *dalit* groups in India are *paraiyas, pulayas, kuravas, chuhras, chamars, mahars, malas* and *madigas*.

James Massey opines about the *dalits* as follows: "They number more than 200 million in our country, and if we include with them the lower sections of Indian society called Backward Classes (OBC) or *shudras*, then the number would be more than 700 million. Among the Indian Christians who number almost 25 million, 75 per cent or more than 20 million, belong to a *dalit* background" (James Massey, ed., *Indigenous People: Dalits*, New Delhi: ISPCK, 1994, p. 4).

## 3. Record of Violence against Dalits

Incidence of violence against scheduled castes (2008) is as follows: In all India, 33615 incidences of crime against *dalits*—Uttar Pradesh (8009), Madhya Pradesh (2965), Rajasthan (4302), Odisha, Gujarat, Bihar, Jharkhand, Andhra Pradesh, Karnataka and Kerala have the record of highest number of crimes against the *dalits*. Murder, rape, hurt, kidnapping and abduction are the common forms of crime or violence against them. There is an increase of violence against *dalits* (The rate of violence or crime against them are increased from 2.6 in 2007 to 2.9 in 2008). A total of 1457 cases of rape of women belonging to *dalit* background were reported in the country as compared to 1349 cases in 2007.

According to Felix Wilfred, the upper and middle caste people inflict violence on *dalits*, and some of the instances are barbaric in nature. Five *dalits* were killed in Jhajjar (Haryana), for skinning a dead cow. In Abohar, Punjab, three *dalit* youth were forced to consume urine. In another incident three *dalit* youth were killed in Saharanpur, UP, because they won a cricket match against the upper caste people. In Thinniam, Thiruchirappalli (Tamil Nadu), two *dalits*—Murukeshan and Ramaswami—where branded with hot iron rods and were forced to feed each other with human excreta (*Dalit Empowerment*, Delhi: ISPCK, 2007. p. 19). In January 2006, a *dalit* by name Bent Singh from Mansa district of Punjab was attacked by upper caste people. He was beaten up and his limbs had to be amputated. The reason is that in 2004 when his eldest daughter was raped by an upper caste Jat, he went to seek justice in court which resulted in conviction of several upper caste people (*Ibid*., p. 23). Sexual violence on *dalit* women by upper caste people is continuing in Uttar Pradesh and other states.

The condition of *dalits* in Kerala is also very pathetic as we see elsewhere in India. Most of the *dalits* live in slums, most of them are landless, so they found shelter in road sides or near the railway tracks. They are neglected by government, the church and the Society. They lack educational and health facilities, shelter, sanitation, water supply and also employment. They are powerless, so their rights are denied. They are forcefully evacuated by the government from their occupied land as they have no title deed. They are unprotected in police stations. There are instances of custodial death as they are not considered as rightful citizens of this country. They are always brutally treated by police.

The diginity of *dalits* are not recognized by the dominant caste in Kerala. They are psychologically and physically tortured. This torture is found in schools, colleges, companies, government and private offices and other work places. Their contributions and abilities are ignored, and their mobility is restricted. In the work place they are considered as slave class. The *dalit* women are also sexually exploited.

### 4. *Tyranny of Ranvir Sena*

The *dalits* have been oppressed by the dominant for many centuries, now, the *dalits* are trying to come out of the oppressive forces like the elitistic/Brahminic dominance and the feudal lords. The *dalits* are organized to guard themselves from exploitation. The feudal lords/landowners of our country do not tolerate the emergence of the *dalits* as a force. So the Ranvir Sena is formed in order to oppress the *dalits*.

The *dalits* were treated as slaves, objects, untouchables and inferior beings by the Brahminic class. They forced to do labour for Rs. 10 or 15 per day. Today the situation is changing because of the growing awareness among the *dalits*. They are conscious of their dignity and rights. The upward mobility and their emergence are understood by the *dalits* as a threat. So the feudal structure is using violence against *dalits* in order to oppress them. Ranvir Sena is a banned organization. They have killed 23 *dalits* in Sankarbega village (23 January, 1999) and 12 *dalits* in Jahanabad (11 January, 1999). The Government of Bihar had failed to find out the culprits. The attacks on *dalits* are continuing. The killings were brutal, ruthless and inhuman. The Ranvir Sena is understood to be formed in order to protect the landlords. It is reported that till date they have killed more than 281 poor villagers. It is to be noted that the Ranvir Sena has deliberately used violence against the *dalits* without any provocation. Few years back they had killed several *dalits* in Lakshmon badhe. The Ranvir Sena should realize that they are playing with fire by involving in the inhuman act of killing innocent *dalit* men, women and children.

It is the prime duty of the Government to protect the *dalits*. It is also important that the *dalits* should organize themselves to curb the violence of Ranvir Sena. An awareness should be created among the people to identity and to respond creatively to the brutal acts of the Ranvir Sena, the *goondas* of the feudal powers.

The *dalits* are the oppressed and marginalized, socially and politically. It is important to realize the need to emancipate the *dalits* from the clutches of unfreedom, injustice and exploitation. The liberation of India is solely depending on the liberation of the *dalits*.

### *5. Dalits as the Oppressed Humanity*

The Indian society, regardless of Christians and non-Christians, the caste system is upheld. Rev. Dr. Alphonsus Mathias, the former Archbishop of Bangalore has rightly said in the 'Foreword' to the book '*Dalit Christian: A Socio-economic Survey*' by Ambrose Pinto, "The Scheduled castes in the country today are in an ambivalent position. Economically, they are the most backward and socially the most retarded. For centuries, they have existed as the most deprived and ostracized people. They have not been permitted to play a significant role in nation-building. Vested interest groups have kept them out in the decision making process of the country. Any attempt to organize them was looked upon with fear and suspicion by upper castes and classes". Caste system is the curse and cancer of Indian Society. The evil of caste system have left no area untouched. It permeates without any reservation. This poison has contributed to socio-economic and political inequality. Because of the centuries long oppression, they are economically retarded, politically weak and psychologically broken. Regret to say that the churches accepted the lordship of the dominant class and caste. The status of a *dailt* as a human being is seriously questioned by the dominant castes. Nobody is here to uplift them and to encourage them. All rights are denied to them. They are not found in the main stream. Many churches are oppressing or closing their door to the *dalits*.

The psychological brokenness is a serious threat. The *dalits* have found it uneasy to move with the dominant because of their inhuman attitudes. Here the question of integration or separation is also very important. The cruelty of discrimination cannot be tolerated all the time. It is human to challenge the unjust structures. It is christian to throw away the structures of inhumanity. The Armageddon is not only on a final catastrophe, but also a daily experience. The evil and injustice are to be challenged and defeated. Christian message is radical and revolutionary. The mission today is nothing other than conscientizing the dominant castes against the prejudices towards the *dalits*. Many theologians are fascinated by the Advaita strand of Indian philosophy. While the vedas and Upanishads have ample references about caste system and its legitimization, how can Advaita be hailed? The problem in Indian theological sphere is that theology is created by the dominant and for the dominant. Theological integrity is not blind accommodation but challenging the evil and falsehood.

The *dalits* are down-trodden. They are not found in the mainstream of the society. Though the major part of Indian population constitute the *dalits*, they have not yet received any recognition. All the crooked ways are used by the powerful to suppress them. In this context the *dalits* of India regardless of their religious affiliations should unite and organize to gain their rights such as liberty and equality. The *dalits* have to wake up from their inferiority feeling and rise to consciousness. They should stop surrendering their dignity to the dominant. The *dalits* are pure race and they are the indigenous people of India. Originally they are Indians. The meaningful co-existence of various communities in India lays its emphasis on equality, fraternity and agapeic love.

The *dalits* also have to develop the feeling of oneness. The plight of the *dalits* is none other than their disunity. Unless they are organized, no liberation is possible for them. The educated and the enlightened *dalits* should try to work for the emancipation of the fellow *dalits*. They should learn to accept and respect each other. They should realize the urgency of their liberation. It is the duty of the *dalits* to struggle for their identity and dignity. The different communities should also be enlightened to change their attitude towards the *dalits*. Socialism, liberty, equality and fraternity cannot prosper in India unless the *dailts* are uplifted. The transformation and development of India cannot be achieved without the development of the *dalits*. The dilemma of *dalits* is the dilemma of India as a nation since *dalits* are the backbone of India.

### *6. The Dalit Christians and Constitutional Rights*

The *dalits* are the oppressed, marginated and voiceless people of India. Anyone who is oppressed is a '*Dalit*' in the broad sense of the term. Since the so called low caste people are oppressed and crushed ruthlessly by the dominant and the term 'dalit' is referred specially in relation to them. They are socially weak, economically backward and politically powerless. The caste system has contributed to the pathetic condition of the *dalits*. They are, now, away from the mainstream of the society. Historically they were alienated for more than five thousand years. This Dravidian community which is scattered in different parts of India, as a result of Aryan suppression, is struggling to come up.

Around fifteen per cent of the *dalits* in India are Christians. It is also observed that around three fourth of the Christians in India are *dalits*. The dalit Christians are thrice oppressed. They are being oppressed by the society, the church and the government. The Simon Commission in 1927 summarized the demands of *dalits* which includes: (1) adequate representation for *dalits* in local, provincial and central legislatures, (2) extension of franchise, (3) safeguarding their education and civil right. Dr. B.R. Ambedkar has considered *dalits* as a separate minority from Hindu community. The question before Simon Commission was whether christian *dalits* should be considered separately or not. The All India Adi-Dravida Jana Sabha argued that the *dalit* can be a depressed one even after becoming a Christian or after conversion.

In should be asserted that whether Hindu or Christian, *dalits* are depressed so religion should not be a barrier to consider them as scheduled castes. We find a discrimination in the constitution itself which goes against the vision of the preamble that affirms the equality, liberty and justice of all, regardless of caste and religion. Articles 14 and 15 of the Constitution do not accept any kinds of discrimination on the ground of religion, race, caste, sex and place of birth.

It is surprising to note that the Government of India Act, 1935 argues that no Indian Christian shall be deemed a member of a scheduled caste. The Constitution has been amended several times to define the scheduled caste. In 1950, the Constitution (Article 314 – which empowered the President to form a list of (scheduled castes) explained that only Hindus are scheduled castes and no other. In 1960, it is defined that the Sikhs, the Jainists and Buddhist can also be recognized as 'Hindu' and they should be included in the scheduled caste list. It is interesting to note that our Constitution has recognized that *dalit* coverts to Jainism, Buddhism and Sikhism. Hindus failed to recognize that the *dalits* convert to Christianity. This discrimination goes against the secularist ideals of our Constitution. What the Christian *dalits* demand is not to recognize them as Hindus, but to consider them as scheduled castes to have their Constitutional rights and privileges.

The *dalit* Christians are an oppressed group of people along with all other *dalits*. So they should get their privileges in the area of employment, education and economic assistance which will enhance their social mobility. Whether Christians, Hindus or Sikhs are *dalits* and they are being oppressed. So the *dalit* Christians also should be constitutionally protected. In the struggle of the *dalit* Christian to get their Constitutional privileges, all the *dalits* should unite. The cause of the *dalit* Christian is the cause of all *dalits*. Sad to say, certain Hindu *dalit* organization are protesting against the inclusion of *dalit* Christians in the scheduled caste list. All *dalits* have to unite in the struggle for their justice. Thanks to the Christian churches which stand firm for the cause of the *dalit* Christians.

### 7. *For a Fair World Order*

In the midst of inequality, exploitation and injustice, the subject of a fair world order has its own significance. Inequality has, somehow, become an integral part of our social structure. The dominant class tries to maintain *status quo* so that the programme of exploitation can be continued. Building up of a just society is the pressing need of today. Even the church as well as the society seem to have ignored the cause of the poor, so their condition remains the same. Unless, the liberation of the poor is a commitment of everybody, the condition of the poor cannot be changed.

The caste system is a psychological, philosophical and physical oppression. The poor in India mainly belong to the so-called lower castes and they constitute the bulk of our population. Their health and educational facilities are not satisfactory. They are oppressed by the dehumanizing social, economical, political and religious system. The instruments of capitalism are regulating all these systems. They live mostly in villages and are alienated from the mainstream of the society.

Even in the matter of medical facilities, the rich enjoy the most sophisticated treatment while the poor have the worst. The poor die without getting proper treatment. According to U.N. Universal Declaration, "everyone has the right to a standard to living adequate for the health and well-being of himself and of his family" (Health Care in India, edited by John Desrochers and *et al.*, p. 3). Compared to urban areas the rural village facilities are very pathetic. Education is only a dream to the poor. There is lack of motivation and opportunity for them to continue their studies. The facilities available to them are very meagre.

The *dalits* (Harijans) of India are a sad lot. They are powerless. Most of them are bonded slaves. The *Dalits* are oppressed and exploited, and are even denied fair wages. They are a voiceless people. They are not allowed to cross the land and houses of high castes. The temple are practically closed to them, even now. The water wells are prohibited to them. Their women are harassed and raped and they are asked to keep away from shops. When the *dalits* are attacked, the police simply close their eyes. They take no action against the assailants. The dominant classes are jealous of their development and educational progress. It is an irony that the historians of our great nation have really ignored the contribution of the *dalits*. Their contribution in the independence struggle and their role in social reform is simply forgotten. The church too has forgotten to record the contribution of the *dalits*. The police has registered fake cases against them, and there are instances in Kerala and Karnataka that the police is alleged to have forcibly made the *dalits* eat human excreta. These kinds of dehumanizing acts are taking place in a civilized country like ours.

The violence against the *Dalits* are increasing everyday. The *dalits* are disorganized, and the time has come for them to get organized. John Kumar has well portrayed the condition of the *dalits* in India. He is of the opinion that their per capita income, is not even rupees two hundred, and many of them go to sleep with empty stomachs. In districts such as Calicut and Wynad, the poor tribals are being deceived by threats and with alcohol, to obtain their land. The History of India is a record of exploitation and systematic violence.

The poor are, after all, suffering everywhere. They are horribly affected by the oppression of the internal and external exploitative elements. The dominant class of the Third World countries are evidently joining hands with the multinationals to exploit the poor. Unless man recovers from the sin of selfishness, it is impossible for them to have a fair world order. The contradiction in our democracy is greatly obvious. India is said to be the largest democratic nation in the world, but it has also degenerated to a large extent. The corrupt bureaucracy of our country has swallowed up most of the developmental programmes and their benefits. They have failed miserably to implement the programmes for the development of the poor. According to Justice Mr. V. R. Krishna Iyer, there cannot be any democracy without justice. The sorry fact is that corruption has become a part and parcel of our structure, from the top to the bottom. Fairness is absolutely absent. Justice Mr. Krishna Iyer say again that a casteless classless society was the dream of those who struggled for independence. But it has dashed to despair after we attained Independence.

### 8. Dalit Emergence

'*Dalit*' means oppressed, crushed, or scattered. They represent the powerless people of India who are the so-called low castes. They are socially, economically and politically alienated. Their rights are denied. In the religious hierarchical order, they are fixed at the end as untouchables. As they are landless and poor they have depend on the land owners or the dominant caste for their survival. Most of them are bond slaves or born slaves. The *Dalit* consciousness has emerged and now they try to organize themselves against the oppressive structures. What Bhim Rao Ambedkar has dreamt will come true in the near future. The *dalits* of India can dream of a good future. Of course, they can have hopes. As the Blacks of North America sang, the *dalits* of India also can sing, 'we shall overcome someday'. So far the dominant classes of India had domesticated the *dalits* of India. The *dalits* could only stay under the shadow of the upper caste. The aspiration of the *dalits* were surrendered to the dominant classes of the India. The voting power of the *dalits* were manipulated by the oppressive classes. The minorities of India like the Muslims, the Sikhs, the Buddhists, the Jainists, the Christians and the oppressed brethren from the Hindu religion should unite together against Brahminical dominance. The five thousand years of upper caste oppression should go. The *dalits* of India should join together disregarding the differences for the great target of demolishing the oppressive structure of India. The *dalits* were burnt, harassed and prevented from progress (educational, socio-economic and political). The dominant classes have used the *dalits* as vote-banks and their privileges were usurped. So far the Brahminical dominance has reigned India by manipulating the *dalit* votes. The *dalits* have been kept away from the mainstream of the society. The greatest poison that still prevails in the Indian society is noné other than the caste system and the resultant exploitation and suppression. The caste system disintegrates, oppresses, dehumanized and departmentalizes the Indian masses. The *dalits* were considered as sub-human. They were not given any importance than a beast. They were used as slaves. They were tortured. The dominant classes of India had the 'privilege' of tapping their labour power and wisdom for their benefit. They never share power and resources to *dalits*. The *dalits* are understood as weak and frail. The emergence of the *dalits* discloses the fact that no one can be suppressed for a long time. The plight of the *dalits* will not stay for ever. The wind of change is very much visible in the Indian Continent. The *dalits* are acknowledged as a significant power in India today. There was a time when the *dalits* could not find any meaning in life. They saw the future as dim. But today there is rays of hopes. The *dalits* should have only one aim, that is to overcome the evil structures which dehumanize them. Paul Lehmann, the American ethicist opined that God is keeping human life human. Yes, the responsibility is to respond to God's act of humanization.

The emergence of the *dalits* is a watershed in the history of India. The misguided religions and political parties are not the great concern of the *dalits*, but their liberation as they respond to God's liberative act. They are no longer bound to a Brahminical God who promotes indignity and inequality. God is siding with the *dalits*, since God is active in history to liberate the oppressed. The evil structures cannot sustain all the time. They may prevail for some time, but would be eventually defeated. The incarnation (Christ event) is for the deliverance of the poor. Jesus was challenging the oppressive elements and he did work for the liberation of downtrodden and outcaste of the day. The real India can come to existence only through the emancipation of the *dalits*. India's hopes can be fulfilled only when the aspiration of the *dalits* is realized. The *dalits* should have the awareness and self determination and they all have to work for their emancipation.

Mahatma Gandhi has called the *dalits* of India as Harijans, the people of God. It is evident that the *dalits* have traditionally worshiped Siva and not Vishnu or Krishna, so they should be called as Sivajans. Today the *dalits* belong topical different religious communities, but their destiny continues to be the same. Dravidians are the original inhabitants of India, but they were suppressed by the Aryan invaders. This suppression and the consequent exploitation and discrimination over *dalits* continue over centuries. The Brahminical dominance became an unquestionable power in the Indian context. Different communities had competed with one another in order to oppress the *dalits*. In Kerala also the Christians who claim the Nambuthiri (Kerala Brahmins) tradition and the Syrian tradition also have shown so much of disparity towards the *dalits*.

## B. Tribal Issues and Responses

The tribal people are the indigenous people who are having a particular geographical area or territory with distinctive culture. They have a particular worldview and behaviour pattern and value system. They are the aboriginal people. In India eight per cent of the population is tribals. The Red Indians and the Maoris are the aboriginals and there are a number of tribal groups in the east and west. They are mostly the forest-dwellers or ' Vanavasis'. They are the people of the land and the early inhabitants. They live by the forest. They call themselves as the sons of soil. The soil and water are sacred to them. Forest is their main source of food. The Adivasis are original inhabitants of a land.

### *1. The Tribal Population*

The major tribes are Abors (Arunachal Pradesh), Angami, Ao (Nagaland) Aptami, Adi (Arunachal Pradesh), Irulas, Kurichiyars, Kurumba (Kerala), Vhails, Gonds (M.P.), Dangs (Gujarat), Santhals (West Bengal, Bihar), Mundas (Bihar) and Khasis (Meghalaya). There are also other tribal groups in India. The tribal people of India are settled in six major areas: North Central India, North East India, South Eastern India, Western India, South India and North India. According to the 1991 Census, the population of scheduled tribes is 6.78 crore, constituting 8.08 per cent of the country's total population. Their literacy rate is just 29.60 per cent compared to the national average of 52 per cent. The tribal population in Kerala is 36,430 (1.14%) as the total population is 3,18,41,374. According to another estimate the *Adivasi* population in Kerala is 1.45 per cent compared to the total population in Kerala and there are around fifty Adivasi groups in Kerala.

The first official reference to classify tribals was found in Government of India Act, 1935 where it is referred 'Backward tribals'. After the existence of Constitution in 1950, the classification of scheduled castes and tribes was made, states Lalrinawmi Ralte [*Religion and Society*, vol. 50 (September 2005), p. 25]. According to N.K. Vaid, "The Constitution of India does not define Scheduled Tribes as such. Article 366(25) refers to Scheduled Tribes as those communities who are scheduled in accordance with Article 342 of the Constitution. This article says that only those communities who have been declared as such by the President, through an initial public notification will be considered as "scheduled tribes" (*who cares for tribal development*. New Delhi: Mittal Publications, 2004, p. 5). The Lokur Committee has identified scheduled tribes having following characteristics: (a) Primitive traits, (b) Distinctive culture, shyness of contact with public at large, (c) Geographic isolation, and (d) Social and economic backwardness (*Ibid.*, p. 6).

According to 1991 Census, the tribal population in the country is 67. 76 million constituting 8.08 per cent of the total population. The literacy rate among them is 29.6 per cent and female literacy among tribals is 18.2 per cent. It falls below the over all literacy rate of the country (52.2%). The Constitution of India guarantees equality in the form of provisions for the advancement of tribals [Article 15(4)], in matters of appointment to any office under the state (Art. 16) and in matters of promotion [Art. 16(4A)]. They are protected from social injustices and exploitation and State is giving special care in their educational and economic interests (Art. 46). Politically, the tribals are having reservation seats in the Parliament (Art. 330), Legislative Assemblies of the States (Art. 332) and in Panchayat (Art. 243 D). The Ministry of Tribal Affairs is constituted in October 1999 for the justice, development and empowerment of tribals (*Ibid.*, pp. 12-13).

### 2. Record of Violence Against Tribes

A total of 5,582 crimes against scheduled tribes were reported in the country during 2008 as compared to 5,532 cases in 2007, showing an increase of 0.9 per cent in 2008 over 2007. There are incidence of murder, rape, kidnapping, abduction and hurt. The reported incidence of violence against tribes during 2008 in all India is 5582. Rajasthan (1038), Madhya Pradesh (1071), Chhattisgarh (614), Andhra Pradesh (750) and Kerala (106) are in the front row in reported crimes against tribes.

In Attappady (Palghat district of Kerala), The 'Attapady Hills Areas Development Society' (AHADS) had acquired the land (3.75 acres owned by an *adivasi* named *kali*) without paying the cost of the land. The government, the windmill company and the land mafia played a deceptive role to acquire the land of tribal people (*Malayala Manorama* (daily) June 29, 2010. p. 4).

There are cases of rape on *adivasi* women reported from Waynad, Calicut and Palghat districts of Kerala. Some *adivasi* girls are allured and are sexually abused; and they become pregnant or having babies before getting married as they are being sexually exploited. The tribal women are also sexually abused by contractors as they offer employment in the area of building constructions and mean jobs in companies. The para-military and military involved in the sexual abuse of tribal women in north eastern states, and Chhattisgarh.

The government is not considering the living condition of the tribes. They suffer from malnutrition, extreme poverty and diseases. The tribal people are found malnourished in Bihar and cases of death by malnutrition is also reported from Nilambur, Malapuram district of Kerala. The police is indiscriminately firing at the tribal people when they protest displacement. This is found at Nandigram (West Bengal) and Kalinga Nagar in South Odisha 13 tribal people where gunned down by police at Kalinga Nagar, as they opposed Tata steel's proposed 6 million tonne steel plant (*The Hindu*, January 3, 2007).

The scheduled tribes chair person Kunwar Singh (2007) observed that the various welfare schemes meant for tribal people are not reaching the target group. He stated that tribes in Kerala are neglected as they are illiterate and tribal hamlets are lacking proper medical facilities, drinking water supply, power and roads. There is also large scale alienation of tribal lands most of the land is not cultivable (*The Hindu*, January 25, 2007). This shows the pathetic condition of the tribal population in Kerala. The systemic violence is very much found in these reports.

In the name of development, the tribal people are disturbed. Their habitat is being destroyed. They are considered as the landless people as they have no legal document. They are chased away without having any concern. Their rights are denied and oppressed. They are exploited as their resources are tapped by these forces. Their humanity is not recognized by them. It is important to uphold their rights and dignity. The Red Indians of United States and the Maories of Australia are almost annihilated by the Whites for the sake of selfish interests.

In India, the lands of tribals are annexed by the dominant class by force or by deception. Their illiteracy, ignorance and innocence are being exploited to gain their goals. They are economically poor and politically powerless, so it is essential to empower them. In the name of development, making of dams and factories, the tribals are forcefully evacuated. They are made landless and powerless and shelterless. In the name of Narmada valley project (in India), around ten lakh tribals are evacuated and they live without proper living conditions.

### *3. The Responses to Tribal Issues*

The government authorities are not serious to take care of their food and health. The famine and diseases are common among the tribals. There is illiteracy and malnutrition. As they are paid low wages, they are not able to improve their living condition.

They should be given their rights over the land, and also they have to be conscientized as to provide guidance to life. It is important to note that the ecological disturbance adversely affect the tribal people.

(1) The Biblical perspective upholds the rights of the marginated including tribal people. Their life is to be safeguarded.
(2) It is the human responsibility to safeguard their land, right and humanity. Never try to disturb their habitat or exploit their resources. The territorial integrity of tribals is to be protected.
(3) The rights of the tribals over the land is to be restored. (In the recent struggles of Kerala Adivasis/tribals under the leadership of C.K. Janu, the Kerala Government had resolved to grant them one to five acres of land). Their privilege should not be grabbed by bureaucracy. It is observed that the term scheduled tribes first appeared in the Constitution of India and Article 366(25) defined it as such tribal communities as are deemed under Article 342 (N.K. Vaid, *Who cares for tribal development*, p. 14).

The tribal people are denied of their identity, dignity and rights. They belong to 'no people' 'no land' category according to the understanding of government and dominant class. The territorial integrity and autonomy are the significant factors for the tribes which are being violated. Their humanity is questioned as they are victimized and their women are sexually exploited. It is unfortunate that they are referred as 'uncultured' and 'uncivilized'. Most of the tribals have become landless bonded labourers. Their privileges are grabbed by the powerful and development is very minimal in the tribal context. Most of the development programmes are to tap their resources and to evacuate them forcefully from their habitat. The recent Nandigram, Singur incidents in West Bengal in the name of

Special Economic Zone and Tata's Nano project is one of the best example for this.

According to Nirmal Minz, the colonial British attitude was not able to appreciate the tribal values. He states "The communitarian ownership of properties, equality among people, democratic organizations and decision by consensus in the administration of law and order, accommodative spirit and the acceptance of all human beings with hospitality, honesty and truthfulness, among the tribal people in India were not accepted as human values by the colonial government and even by our national government in our country" ["Tribal Issues in India Today", *Religion and Society*, Vol. 50, No. 3 (September 2005), pp. 6-7].

Nirmal Minz continues to opine that the Government of India has officially denied the existence of indigenous tribal people in India and Government of India do not want the *Adivasis* to continue as a distinct people in this country (*Ibid.*, p. 8). Government of India and also some sociological theorists like G.S. Ghurye, he states, who are looking forward the assimilation of the tribals into the main stream of the society (*Ibid.*, p. 8).

These are the threatening situation of the identity of the tribal people as they are objectifying and dehumanizaing tendencies. The Government of India and society should not nullify the emergence and empowerment of the tribals. Their future has to be bright as they live as a people with identity, dignity and rights. Sangh Parivar does like to refer tribal people as *Vanavasis* (Forest-dwellers) than *Adivasis* (original inhabitats) in order to reduce the *Adivasis* to a people without a history, states Santanu Patro (*Religion and Society*, vol. 50, September 2005, p. 12). This is also a threat to their identity and status. The fundamentalism and pseudo secularism which insist on a single religion, culture and ideology is also a threat to the pluralistic foundation of our nation and to the identity of *dalits* and *Adivasis*. It reduces the religious minorities, *dalits* and *Adivasis* as second class citizens (*Ibid.*, p. 17).

The Sangh Parivar will also deny the identity, dignity and rights of minorities and subaltern groups. Hinduism is used by

Brahminic forces and Sangh Parivar as an umbrella under which they nurture caste system or Varnashrama Dharma to uphold their dominance. The recent incidents (2008) in Orissa, the Sangh Parivar used tribals against Christian tribals for their interest.

The land is life for the tribal people which is robbed from them by the British colonizers, the zamindars and other dominant communities. They also became landless as the land is taken by force or evacuated them from it by the government authorities. The land is lost and become landless labourers. The immigrants also grabbed the tribal land by deceptive means. According to P. Alexendar, they are also exploited by the selfish traders and greedy moneylenders (*Ibid.*, p. 42). They had to surrender their properties and land for their loans to these people. The tribals are also forced to become bonded labourers (*Ibid.*, p. 43).

It is the responsibility of the church, society, government and voluntary organizations to work for the development and liberation of the tribes. These sincere people should be protected from social, economic, political and sexual exploitation. Politically, they have to be brought to the main stream of the society by ensuring their participation in decision-making. They should be considered with justice.

God is just and Bible stands for the liberation of the marginalized. The identity, dignity, rights and liberation of the victimized or the subaltern is upheld by the Bible (Ex. 3:7, 10). Israelites were the tribal group who were oppressed and exploited by Egyptians, where God responds to their cry and liberated them. God does have solidarity with the poor, aliens and those who cry for their identity, dignity and rights (Isa. 58: 6-7; Am. 5:12, 24; Lk. 4: 16-21). The conscientization and mobilitization of the tribals is important to gain their rights. The different kinds of exploitation by immigrants, bureaucracy and the landlords have to be stopped.

## C. Response to Inhumanity Against Dalits and Tribes

I was attending a seminar on *dalit* issues where Prof. K.N.

Panikkar, the historian was also present. I also presented a paper on the crisis of *dalits*. When the meeting was over, a pastor asked me, 'whether you have the experience of salvation?' (He did not know anything about my background). He thought the presentation on *dalits* is not something 'spiritual'. This is the attitude of many Christians on *dalit* and tribal issues. So it is important to create an awareness among the people on issues related to *dalits* and tribes. Most of the church members are not concerned of the issues of the victimized in the church and in the society. If they are aware also, they are silent or ignore them

The churches and civil society should initiate the organising and mobilising of the *dalits* and tribal people. M.M. Thomas argued for mobilising the rural and urban poor. Dr. B.R. Ambedkar talks about education, organising and agitation. The spirituality of combat is very important over here. The churches should have the prophetic consciousness to protest the structural evil which is found as violence against *dalits* and tribal people.

In the cases where the churches as a whole divide and fail to stand for the cause of the *dalits* and tribal people, the interest groups and action groups (NGOs) can take up the struggle against the victimistion of *dalits* and tribes. Liberation is possible only through struggles, and it does not come automatically. As M.M. Thomas has pointed out one of the hindrances to a just society is the bureaucratic correction. It is important to fight for the identity, diginity and rights of the marginalised.

The land acquisition by government, private companies and the land mafia is affecting the *dalits* and tribal people. They acquire the land, the habitat of tribal people and *dalits*, by force or by paying a low amount. The neocolonial (Globalisation) forces and their programmes such as MNCs and the special economic zone have created fear and insecurity among *dalits* and tribal people, as they are the first or easy victims of there are agendas. The powerless people are exploited by their forces.

In the name of development the *dalits* and tribal people are forcefully evacuated, which is a severe crime against them. This is happened in Sardar Sarovar Project (SSP) which lead to

Naranda Valley Andolan, and also the struggles in Singur and Nandigram. In Kerala the *dalits* and tribals occupied the Chengara rubber plantations in oder to protest the negligence of government towards the landless. The Kerala Government at last decided to rehabilitate them. When former Chief Minister of Kerala distributed patta (title deed) to Chengara agitators at Pathanamthitta (August 2010), after receiving patta one old woman asked 'where we should go with this?' The Chief Minister puzzled for a moment and then said, 'you may go where the land is'. The document is not specific and it expresses the fact that the meaningful survival of this people in any derelict area (land) is not possible, a proper rehabilitation is not done. This is what happens in most of the cases. The name of rehabilitation *dalits* and tribal people are forcefully sent to the places where there is no facilities to survive. The right to education, employment, shelter, food and land are important for their meaningful survival denying these privilages is a violence against them, which should be curved. The Narmada Valley Andolan and Chengara land struggle have become historic as it asserts the rights of *dalits* and tribal people.

The *dalits* and tribes are to be empowered to attain their rights. The ecumenical network is important tom respond to the issues of violence against *dalits* and tribes. The secular ecumenism of M.M. Thomas and the wider ecumenical understanding promoted by Rev. M.A. Thomas did play a significant role to bring people of all religions and ideologies to actively participate in the cause of the victimised. This is found in a superb manner in Narmada valley, Wayanad and Chengara. The names such as Baba Amte, Medha Patkar, C.K. Janu and Laha Gopalan are worth mentioned over here. The vision of ecumenism-reconciliation, unity and just community was expressed by Christian and non-Christian leaders and activists and people from different ideologies. This solidarity is the expression of real ecumenism.

## Conclusion

*Dalits* and tribal people are the most victimized groups. They are the victims of several forms of violence found in the society. Socially, economically and politically they are discriminated. Their territorial autonomy and integrity are being questioned as they are forcefully evacuated in the name of development. They are the victims of deforestation, ecological disasters and physical torture. Fake cases are registered against them and their rights are denied by authorities. Their diginity is questioned. Though they are the original inhabitants of India, their indigenous people are aliened from land and other resources. No proper facilities are provided to them. They have to survive in the undeveloped areas. So, it is important to emancipate the people from their situations.

# 4

# A Theological and Ethical Reflection for Developing an Eco-Theology

A critical look into the resources, ideology, value system and existing theologies is needed to formulate an eco-theology.

## I. Hermeneutical Process from an Eco-perspective

In the hermeneutical process in relation to ecology, the hermeneutical circle is an important aspect. We have our pre-suppositions about Biblical texts. We have to move from there to the original context and the present context. It is important to redeem ourselves from our traditional, imperialistic, colonial, domineering view on creation. It is a dialogical and dialectical process.

The 'hermeneutics of suspicion' and ideological criticism and suspicion are also important factors. Though these are very much used in feminist hermeneutics and theology and also in liberation hermeneutics and theology, they are very useful in eco-hermeneutics. We have to suspect the interpretation of the texts, and the formation of ideology which affirm the exploitation of natural resources and destroying the creation. We have to challenge the mafia hermeneutics and mafia ideology which justify consumerism, reckless tapping of resources and polluting the creation.

Inter-textuality is also an important factor. We have to consider the cultural and religious resources which are available in our context. It can include the folklores, songs, poetry, symbols and religious scriptures. It is a post-colonial understanding of what is native and indigenous. The liberative elements from our own resources have to be identified in the hermeneutical process. The spirit of preservation and conservation are found in our own cultural and religious resources (e.g., *'Ahimsa'*, *'Aparigraha'*, *'Jiva'*, *'Karuna'* etc).

The 'Deconstruction' of post-modernism is also helping us to interpret text and reality from a difference (difference), a new angle. A radical challenge to existing ideology and theology of manipulation has to be affirmed. The resources, systems, values and ideas that are anti-ecological have to be deconstructed. The capitalistic, consumeristic and profiteering ideologies have to be reconceived. The reader-response is very important in this new construction.

Reading the text and ideologies from the perspective of the marginalized is another concern. The text has to be liberated from the spirit of oppression. The domination, subjugation and manipulation are to be challenged. It is important to recognize how our interpretations are true to the text and how it affects the people who are marginated. The response of the people and their experience are to be considered. The justice, kingdom of God, just community, and humanness are very important elements to be regarded.

In the hermeneutical process, it is important to reflect the ecological concerns from the themes of the Bible. The creation, covenant, shalom, justice, kingdom of God, creation, incarnation, cross and resurrection, the new earth and new heaven provide clues and resources for doing theology from ecological perspective. The concept of preservation, conservation, the sanctity of environment and the pro-life perspectives are found in the themes. The right to live or survive, co-existence and pro-existence, harmonious existence and cosmotheandric spirituality and vision are integral in this themes. Ecological consciousness and eco-justice are the spirit of these themes. God is concerned of the integrity of creation.

Theology is the critical and creative reflection on faith in the context of the realities and experience around us. Christian ethics is also the critical and creative reflection of our faith in the context of realities and experiences around us focusing on praxis.

We also need theological and ethical affirmations to have an adequate eco-theology. Eco-theology is the critical and creative reflection of our faith in the context of the reality of ecological problems and eco-injustices around us.

(a) We should have the determination to challenge the capitalistic tendencies. The industrialization and market economy are doing lot of harm to our environment. It is related to massive exploitation of resources, and emission of oxides and other toxic gases. The nuclear waste is another danger. For the use of fuel and energy, the wind, sea waves and solar are the options. Use the renewable energy. So also promote liquefied natural gas (LNG) and comprised natural gas (CNG).

(b) We should have the determination to challenge consumerist ideology. Preservation and conservation and the responsible use of energy and other resources is a very important thing to keep up. Market and production control the human beings. There is uncontrolled consumption of food, uncontrolled use of electronic and electric devices and uncontrolled use of resources (water, fuel, minerals etc.).

(c) We should have the determination to protect our environment. Keep our environment clean. Domestic waste, industrial waste (chemical waste) emissions of automobiles plastics, electronic waste, and nuclear waste make our environment polluted. Unselfish, non-possessive and sacrificial attitude is important to have a spirit of care, love and support. The ethics of care and love are significant in this respect. We have to responsibly use the resources. Find appropriate and eco-friendly ways to dispose the waste.

(d) We should have determination to develop an eco-friendly attitude. If we love creation, we care it. We love trees, flora and fauna, the animal kingdom and plant kingdom, and we protect our diverse resources. We will nurture the creation. We should avoid mafia culture and attitude. We should develop an eco-friendly spirituality.

## Biblical and Theological Foundations for an Eco-theology

Following are the Biblical, theological and ethical formulations. Genesis account (1:24-31) talks about God who created the plants and creatures which express the fact that it is not only man, but all plants and creatures have the right to live on this planet. Irresponsible killing of animals, felling of trees and destroying the bio-diversity is anti-human, anti-creation, and anti-God. There is a triangular/trinitarian relationship between God, man and creation.

Protecting wild life, environment and bio-diversity is to be seriously taken care. The ethics of care is a great concern here. Bible begins with ecological concerns. Integrity of creation has to be upheld. Our resources are to be preserved with the perspective that it is deposited for the use of the coming generations also. So we should not have the mafia spirit.

God is the source of life. Life springs from God. God is green (ecologically concerned and eco-friendly). Creation is to be green. God created everything as good, or life in-fullness but because of the broken relationship with God and creation, life-fullness is lost. The sanctity of environment is also lost, as there is manipulation and exploitation of resources. The sanctity of creation and life has to be regarded highly as God has found the creation, good.

The 'kinship' is what our relationship should be with the creation (Gen. 1:29-31). Felix Wilfred suggests 'kinship' than stewardship in his book 'Margins'. The Hebrew word 'Rid' is not to dominate or manipulate, but shepherding. It is to care, protect, preserve and maintain. It is a pastoral imagery than a military or mafia imagery. The shepherds are not to exploit, or to kill but to protect them and to pastor them. Kinship does not permit consumerism. Responsible use of resources, considering the life and well-being is promoted. Today's ideology of pleasure, consumerism and greed are anti-ecological. We should have an anti-greed attitude.

It is also important to note that the Canberra Assembly of W.C.C. (1991) has stressed the work of Holy Spirit in the whole of creation. The theme was 'Come Holy Spirit, Renew the whole creation'. The next WCC (2013) in Busan, South Korea, is based on the theme 'God of life-lead us to peace and justice'. These are ecological themes, which affirm the integrity of creation.

'Okos' and 'Logos' are combined in ecology. It is our home, the whole creation including the earth. Earnst Hackel was the proponent of this term ecology. Lynn white was questioning Judeo-Christian understanding of creation. This American historian has written a very disturbing article 'the historical roots of our ecological crisis' in 1967. He comes to the conclusion that Judeo-Christian theology is fundamentally capitalistic in nature as it supports the exploitation of the earth. He points to the anthropocentrism and domination in the Judeo-Christian theology.

Sallie McFague in 'Metaphorical theology' states that we can no longer see ourselves as rulers over nature but must think of ourselves as gardeners, caretakers, stewards, trustees, lovers, priests, and friends of a world that, while giving us life and sustenance, also depends increasingly on us in order to continue both for itself and for us (pp. 20-21).

Jurgen Moltmann tries to relate the justice concern with ecology. In his words, 'we shall be able to achieve social justice without justice for natural environment; we shall not be able to achieve justice for nature without social justice.'

Romans 8:18-25 talks about the liberation of the creation. Creation looks forward its ultimate redemption and renewal. The 'new earth' is portrayed in the book of revelation. Man is also included in this process. It is a 'theosis' in the perspective of church fathers and the orthodox churches. There is also a reference about cosmic dimension of reconciliation in the epistle of Colossians (1:20). Jesus also said that He came to give life and life in abundance (Jn. 10:10). Jesus was eco-friendly as he used the imageries from the nature to explain the concept of the kingdom of God. He also gave extreme importance to life in fullness or the sanctity of life.

Dr. K.C. Abraham talks about three models of the church in relation to ecology. They are: (a) ascetic-monastic model where renunciation is the key. Greed is understood as the source of the problem of ecology. Here our life style is also important. Monastic ideals can inspire us to have harmonious relationship with nature. (b) Sacramental/Eucharistic model–life and all its relationships are brought to the worshipful presence of God and they are constantly being renewed. We have to recover the dynamic character of eucharist and motivate people to be open to God's creation and recreation. (c) Liberative-solidarity model—according to this model, the church is in solidarity with the weakest, with that part of the creation that is victimized, seeks the renewal of the whole creation. There is an affirmation of the liberation that is witnessed in the Bible includes liberation for creation. The work of the Holy Spirit is to renew all of the earth. We are committed not only in our relationship with one another, but also our relationship with the whole of creation (*Eco-Justice*, Bombay: BUILD, n.d., pp. 23-27). Dr. K.C. Abraham proposes a liberative-solidarity model which is seriously committed to the struggles of justice for the marginated and the exploited nature.

Dr. George Mathew Nalunnakal (presently Metropolitan Gheevarghese Mar Coorilos) proposes a Kenotic spirituality which is a response to eco-crisis. It enables us to resist the greed and consumerism. It is also a help to challenge the capitalistic tendencies which are exploiting the nature and the resources with selfish interests. His book 'Green Liberation' is a response to ecological problems.

I have also developed an 'Agape Tyaga model' (based an 'agape' and *tyaga* or sacrifice and renunciation) in order to respond to eco-problems. It is a cosmo-theandric spirituality which makes use of the resources which are Christian and Indian (The Indian concepts like *Ahimsa, Aparigraha, Tyaga* and *Karuna*). The 'Agape-Tyaga' model (Love and Sacrifice or Renunciation) will help to have eco-friendly perspective which is anti-greed, anti-possessive and anti-exploitative. It will also help to love nature and the whole of creation. Our eco-spirituality should be rooted in love, justice, renunciation and anti-greed and non-egoism. Sebastian Kappen's 'theandric practice' is also important to deal with non-humanizing and oppressive elements which harm the creation. In this connection, the Indian concepts such on *Ahimsa*, *Aparigrarha* and *Anicca* are significant.

The liberation and praxis are also significant over here. The role of social movements such as 'Narmada Valley Andolan' 'Green peace movement', 'Chipko movement' and other ecological movements, so also the civil society movements and social action groups are also playing important roles in the theological process in relation to eco-theology. The eco-justice is a concern over here. The integrity of creation is regarded. It is a liberative process and a liberative praxis, as these movements struggles in a dynamic sense against oppressive structures which are anti-ecological. There is also a solidarity of the people and action groups which are people's movements which includes people from different religions and ideologies with a common cause. So there is a liberative axis in this eco-theological concerns.

The *dalit* and tribal view on nature and the creation is also an important dimension in ecology and eco-theology. The women are also to protect the creation, especially the subaltern women. For the marginated people, land, forest and water are life. They live and survive by the forests. When their habitat is lost, their means of survival is also lost. They live close to the nature and in their worldview creation plays a central role. They have a principle of integration in relation to creation, than the disintegration. There is no secular and sacred distinction or dichotomy in tribal and *dalit* world view. According to Nirmal Minz, "the tribal people's ethic is the ethics of conservation as against the ethics of disruption and destruction of nature of the modern people" ("Tribal perspectives on ecology", (*The Tribal Wordview and Ecology,* edited by A. Wati Longchar and Yangkahao Vashum, Jorhat: Tribal Study Centre, 1998. p. 5). The oral and written traditions, folklores and poems affirm the sanctity of environment which give utmost importance to land, water, trees, plants and animals, which are integral part of their life. The *dalit* and tribal women are also the agents of protection and preservation as they realize that creation is an integral element of life, so they are for protecting the land, river (water), fuel (energy) and other resources from pollutions and exploitations.

Jurgen Moltmann talks about the harmonization between human civilizations and the earth's ecosystems. The goal is not human domination over nature, but it is a well-judged and prudent conformity with nature. It is based on Albert Schweitzers understanding of 'reverence for life' as the foremost commandment which follows from the right to life (*Science and Wisdom,* London: SCM Press, 2003, p. 29). He again states that 'The ecological crisis caused by the progressive destruction of nature has been brought about by Christianity and science jointly; and if human beings and nature want to win a chance to survive in this face of this crisis, Christianity and science must together revise their picture of human being—both the view reflected in the traditional belief in creation. 'Subdue the earth', Gen. 1:28 (*Ibid*., p. 34).

Eco-feminism is also an important dimension in eco-theology. This term was coined by Francoise d' Eaubonne, a French feminist in 1974. Eco-feminists see connections between exploitation and degradation of the natural world and the domination and oppression of women and they trace this to a shared history of oppression by the patriarchal culture [*Jeevadhara* Vol. XL, No. 235 (January 2010), p. 51]. According to Kochurani Abraham, "Eco-feminists see an urgency for uprooting the capitalist patriarchal world system which is built upon and maintained through the colonization of women, of foreign peoples, their land and of nature" (*Ibid*., p. 52).

Sallie Mac Fague in her book '*Models of God: Theology for an Ecologically Nuclear Age*' states that the current symbols of God are inadequate as they provide only a distorted understanding about the relationships among the living beings. So she replaces it by 'Lover', 'Friend', and 'Mother' to depict God, which are anti-hierarchical and anti-patriarchal. For Aruna Guanadason, '*Sakti*' is more than energy. It is also feminine energy, which is the source of all things, both human ('*Purusha*') and non-human ('*Prakriti*' or nature). This feminine divine energy makes the relationship between humanity and rest of creation a sacramental one, and hence must be at the heart of a vision of a new world order (*Green Liberation*, pp. 151-152).

According to Rosemary Radford Reuther, "Sexism and ecological destructiveness are related in the symbolic patterns of patriarchal consciousness, but they also take intensive socio-economic form in modern industrial society. Rapid industrialization went hand in hand with the depletion of the economic functions of women traditionally centred around the home. Industrialization drew also many poor women into the factory at exploitative wages, far below those even of the exploited male worker" (*New Woman New Earth: Sexist ideologies and human liberation*, New York: Seabury Press, 1983, p. 196). In her view, "women must see that there can be no liberation for them and no solution to the ecological crisis within a society whose fundamental model of relationships continues to be one of domination" (*Ibid*., p. 204). She continues to state that the concept of domination of nature has been based on the social domination between master and servant groups, starting with the basic relationship between men and women. An ecological revolution, she says, must overthrow all the social structures of domination (*Ibid*., p. 204).

Sallie Mc Fague, in her book "*Metaphorical Theology: Models of God in Religious Language*" (Philadelphia: Fortress Press, 1982) states that feminists are saying that the particular problem they have with Western religious language is its patriarchal character.

The patriarchal nature is found in the term 'God the father' (p. 9). There is a suggestion of new models in language as God is referred an 'parent', 'love' and 'friend' which can overcome subordination, hierarchy and patriarchal authoritarianism. Parental imageries both parental and natural, are to be used with the notes of compassion, acceptance discipline, forgiveness, nurture' and guidance (p. 177). As male and female experience is not exhausted by parenthood (many are not parents or not planning to become parents) so the balanced, non-gender, non-familial metaphor can be 'God, the friend' (p. 178). God is a friend of humanity (Iraneus of Lyons), and God as fellow-sufferer (A.N. Whitehead). Friendship leads to an ideal, responsible and mature relationship with God. As a friend, God co-operates with humanity to work for the fulfilment of all creation. She states that the friendship model emphasizes sacrifice, support, and solidarity with others and the world (p. 186).

# 5
# The Concept of Justice in the Tirukkural

The Kural (Tirukkural) is a classical Tamil poetry composed by Tiruvalluvar. The scholars have diverse opinion about the period of this classical Tamil Poetry. According to P.S. Sundaram, "It is not easy to fix the date of Kural. Scholars placed it anywhere between the second century B.C. and the eight century A.D." (*The Kural.* New Delhi: Penguin Books, 1990, p. 8). It consists of 1330 couplets dealing with principles of justice, wealth and happiness, says M. Muthuraman in his book entitled "*Religion of Tirukkural*". He again says in his book *Gita and Kural* that "the three major divisions of the work are so well arranged beginning with the principle of justice, that it clearly shows how the principle of justice—the ideal perfection of human relationship—is the basis of the entire work". B. Natarajan recognized the Kural as the 'work of ethics par excellence'.

Justice is integral to the teachings of the Kural. Tiruvalluvar can be recognized as a social reformer in this respect. In the words of Ramanlal Shah, "He (Tiruvalluvar) gave his immortal literary work 'Tirukkural' which has till now inspired generation after generation, particularly in the southern part of India, in their social, economic, political, cultural and religious life" (*First all India Tirukkural Research Seminar papers* (May 1972) edited by N. Sanjeevi, Madras, University of Madras 1973, p. 11). It is quite obvious that he was against the caste discriminations and was for the dignity of all human beings. Tiruvalluvar states, in his thirtieth couplet,

Call them Brahmins who are Virtuous
And kind to all that live.

For him, those who does good and kind are Brahmins. He interprets the word 'Brahmin' in a very revolutionary way. According to B. Natarajan, "It is, of course, needless to tell that valluvar does not in the least tolerate the least difference among mankind on the basis of race." (*Tirukkural Lectures 1950-90 to 1968-69,* p. 646).

Tiruvalluar was deadly against the ill-got wealth and the partiality. He advises that

Wealth ill-got, however useful,
should not be touched.

P.S. Sundaram quotes the rendering of this 113 couplet by Justice M.M. Ismail as follows:

Avoid at once even the good
brought by evil means.

Tiruvalluvar states the same fact in the couplet 754

Wealth acquired sinless and well
Yield both virtue and happiness.

Tirukkural does not entertain any "good" or "blessing" obtained by unjust means. This would certainly imply that Tirukkural is totally against bribery and exploitation. It also warned of any thought on inequity in the couplet 116. He has strongly felt that the injustice is an attitude. Couplet 209 is very closer to Jesus' teaching. The Couplet goes like this:

If you love yourself
Refrain from ill to others.

The teaching of Jesus goes as follows:

'Love your neighbour as thyself.' (LK 10:27)

The teaching of Jesus Christ is that do not do evil to others. Doing evil or ill to others is an act of hatred. We are supposed to accept the dignity of all, and we should not involve in any dehumanizing act. If we don't like anybody to do injustice against us, why we should do injustice to others? The Kural wants everybody to respect and love each other, and to live in equality and justice. Human beings have to refrain from the act oppression of any kind. We should recognize the fact that the structural violence of any sort has the root in our selfish attitude.

According to Tiruvalluvar, justice is one of the hallmarks of any virtuous king. The couplet 390 reads like this:

> A light among kings is he who has
> Grace, Bounty, Justice and Concern.

The kings are known for their luxury and oppression. They are after pomp and glory at the expense of the poor. Here the kural has counted the virtue of any king in terms of one's act of Justice. The 'impartial eye' and 'justice' are again emphasized by Tirvalluvar in couplets 541, 542, and 548. He imprecates the unjust kings in couplet 548.

> A King inaccessible, unprobing and unjust
> will sink and be ruined.

This reflects how much Tiruvalluvar's mind was after justice. He does not compromise with any injustice. He strongly condemns the 'sinful and oppressive' kings in couplet 551.

> A sinful and oppressive king is worst
> than a murderer.

He compares the oppressor with a murderer. The act of oppression is a murder for Tiruvalluvar. His sense of justice is certainly commendable. He says in couplet 994 as follows:

> The world loves the gentility which combines
> Justice with benevolence.

Tiruvalluvar has understood injustice as an attitude of mind as well as a structural reality. According to M. Muthuraman, 'in Tirukkural mention has been made of the supremacy of justice as the guiding principle of life and death' (*Religion of Tirukkural*, p. 21). He also argues that Tirukkural asked to accept the dignity of fellow human beings, brotherhood and equality (*Religion of Tirukkural*, p. 55). Tirukkural looks forward the happiness in life which is rooted in fairness or justice. Justice is very inevitable for fair human relationships. This fact is affirmed by Tirukkural. Justice is the overarching theme in Tirukkural. It is justice which integrates all other virtues. The virtues like love, kindness and charity are grounded on justice in Tiruvalluvar's perspective. Tirukkural's ethical thought is based on justice which foresees a world without exploitation and discrimination.

# 6
# The Legal Action-Guide and Religious Pluralism
## A Methodological Perspective

### Introduction

Religious pluralism is one of the main issues in the recent theological discussions. There are different religious traditions and cultural diversities in the world. It means that there are different customs, religious beliefs and practices. The diverse cultural and religious contexts bring diverse beliefs, taboos, customs, morals and rules. The various religious traditions have their own beliefs and ethical principles.

The exclusive claims of the religions cause great concern in the religiously plural society. The religious fundamentalism is areal danger to peaceful co-existence. It is quite obvious that when different religious groups stay together in a society, it is impossible to use an absolute rule or law on a group. All religions have provided a religious action guide for those who have faith in a particular religion. When people from two religions conflict on an issue. The two action-guide. In the religiously plural society two factors can conflict. The conflict can be between the two religious action-guide.

This chapter is an attempt to see what are the methodological issues involved regarding the legal action-guide in the pluralistic society. And this will also try to formulate some suggestions toward a law or legal action-guide that can be valid and acceptable to all.

## I. Legal Action-Guide: An Explanation

Christian ethics or ethics in general is concerned with the rules, norms or the law of the society. According to Little and Twiss, the legal action-guides are based on a sovereign authority and it is a system of action-guides to settle the disputes, reinforce norms and regulate transactions (David Little and Sumner B. Twiss, *Comparative Religious Ethics*, New York: Harper & Row Publishers, 1978. p. 84). At this point, it is important to identify the difference between the religious action-guide and legal action-guide. While the religious action-guide is the issue of commands, edicts and orders by the sacred authority, the legal action-guide is the commands, duties or rules which controls human behaviour in the society. According to David Little and Summer Twiss, the legal action-guide is hardly intrinsically religious, at the same if the sacred and legal action-guide can be one and the same if the sacred and legal sovereign is one and the same (*Ibid.*, p. 93). The latter can take place only in a uni-religious society (e.g. some Islamic countries).

In the words of Little and Twiss, "All institutions are composed of customs. Some customs are reinstitutionalized at a higher level so to speak. They are restated for the purpose of achieving security of the social order and related ends. When they are so restated or reinstitutionalized, these customs are raised to the status of law and constitute yet another superintending institution (*Ibid.*, p. 78). They took a legal statement to be statement expressing the acceptance of an action-guide that claims superiority and that is considered legitimate and in that it is justifiable and evokes a notion of sovereign authority that is at once normative and effective (acknowledged and enforced by officials) (*Ibid.*, p. 85).

The understanding of W.J. Rees is also quite significant over here. According to him, "Laws can only be effectively administered if there exists some final legal authority beyond which there is no further legal appeal. In the absence of such a final authority no legal issue could ever be decided (*Ibid*., p. 80). For Little and Twiss, a legal sovereign is a supreme norm, or agent which has authority, as a matter of right, over all other institutions, action-guides or persons within the legal system."

The law or legal action-guide consists of two elements, the primary rules (restraints) and secondary rules (enforcement). Without the secondary rules the primary rules can't stand, and it will be reduced to a moral action-guide. According to Westminster Dictionary of Ethics, there is God-made law (revelation), human made law (legislators) and temporal law (customs), (James F. Childress and Macquarie, the West Minster Dictionary of Ethics, Philadelphia: The West Minster Press, 1973, p. 342).

In the following discussions, God given or revealed law may be seen separate from the human-made and temporal. The components of law can be customs and reason.

## II. Methodological Issues

There are so many issues in the context of religious pluralism. The main issue for our consideration from the point of view of the law or legal action-guide is the conflict for supremacy between religious action guide and legal action-guide. The assumption is that the legal action-guide is consisted of customs (temporal law), the human-made law (legislators/parliament/legal experts) and probably the natural law (reason). The law is always meant for all people in a society regardless of religions. When two religious communities confront, the law intervenes there. It has to intervene to accomplish the purpose of settling the disputes and controlling the social behaviour. This is where the religious communities can become fundamentalistic or fanatic and challenge the legal sovereign.

This happens when the religious action-guide conflict with legal action-guide. The religious communities look up to their priests or other sacred authority and obey them regardless of the existing laws. In the context of religious pluralism, the issue is that when the conflict between religious action-guide and legal action-guide arise the priority usually with the religious action-guide.

Another issue can be the conflicting opinions about the religious action-guide within a religious community, and it may be challenged because of the awakening through modernization and secularization. Here the role of the legal action-guide becomes very crucial. The same religious community may fall apart when the legal sovereign makes judgements over some issues.

Yet another issues may be the conflicts arise when legal action-guide challenges the religious action-guide. Here the law tries to take priority over religious action-guide. It will also cause conflicts. The issues are interlinked since in the context, the conflict is mainly between the religious action-guide and legal action guide. Not only that the role of legal action-guide is very crucial in all these issues.

In Islam the "Shariah" is the integral part of the word of Allah. It is also eternal and universal for Islam. It sets forth and regulates man's obligations to man and God, and Islam believes that Allah's all commandments—ritual and civil—are recorded in *Quran* (Philip K. Hitti, *Islam: A way of life*, Minneapolis, University Minnesota Press, 1969, p. 42). In the *Shah Bano* case the verdict of the Supreme Court was challenged by the fundamental Muslims and Muslim scholars. The issue has created some problems within the religious action-guide or the Personal Law of Islam. Here law made a decision, but was challenged by a group within that religious community.

One of the prominent consequences of *Jihad* (Holy War) can be said as the conflict between two religious communities. In this situation, the legal action-guide has to settle the problem. This can be a confrontation between the legal action-guide and religious action-guide for affirming their superiority.

The question of '*Sati*' is another issue. Though the law is against any kind of killing or murder or even against suicide, the

Rajputs (Rajasthan) and some religious communities in West Bengal are practicing it. Even after the injunctions of the court of law, it was continued. Here religious action-guide takes priority over the legal action-guide.

The law or legal action-guide can be against the discrimination against women, but the religious fundamentalists find their refuge in their religious scriptures or religious action-guide. The *Manusmriti* is used for supporting the discrimination against women. The religion *versus* law conflict was evident in the "Operation Blue Star" (Khalistan issue in Punjab) and Babri-Masjid issue.

### *III. A Legal Action-Guide for the Context of Religious Pluralism*

There may not be any absolute ideas behind this discussion. This is an attempt to see, in the light of the methodological issues raised, what can be the criterion used to have a legal action-guide for the context of religious pluralism?

There are personal laws for all religions. Or we may say there is an action-guide for all religions. Or we may say there is an action-guide for all religious communities. In India, there are civil codes for all religious groups. Few years ago, the Christian inheritance law was challenged by Mary Roy. This case and Shah Bano case challenge the religious communities to have a rethinking within them. In the *New Testament*, we read that Jesus was challenging the legalism of Judaism. Legalism is the rules without love and human concern. According to Joseph Fletcher, this legalism is the love of law rather than the law of love.

The Ramjanmabhoomi-Babri Masjid issue is quite alive in India for some time. This issue is between two religious communities. Religious leaders were even tried to violate the injunctions of the legal authority. None of the communities were willing to yield in this issue. Will they obey the court?

The severe problem which is confronted by the law is that the religious communities are operated by their sentiments and they are least bothered about what is right, good and responsible.

I would like to make some suggestions at this point to form a criteria to decide on the conflict between religious and legal action-guide. These are not very exclusive, but open to questions.

1. The existing religious action-guide and legal action-guide should be reviewed in the light of what is human. It can be done through a dialogue and objective study.
2. What is humane can be the question of equality, justice, human rights and sensibility.
3. A new religious and legal action guide should be formed by incorporating the good elements from the secular and sacred realm.

While discussing on the issue of a uniform civil code in India, A.B. Shah has made some suggestions.

1. A uniform civil code should not be an extension of Hindu code to other communities.
2. The new code should corporate the good elements from all the personal laws currently in force in India.
3. It should be based on the fundamental rights in the constitutions regardless of sex or creed (A.B. Shah, *Religion and Society in India*, New Delhi; Somaiya Publications, 1981, p. 119).

It is well and good if it works in the pluralistic context. But will the absolute claims of religious fundamentalists accept this? If the human rights are acceptable as the criteria for the examination of religious action-guide and legal action-guide, that can be a real revolution in this respect. It will enable to form a legal action-guide and religious action-guide on the basis of human rights. A renewal on the basis of human rights would be a real challenge for the religious and legal action-guide. The issue between legal action-guide and religious action-guide can be resolved only by turning away from the legalism and selfish interests [V.K. Sinha (ed), the *Secularist* (No. 122) March-April,

p. 39]. Religious action-guides also should have a quest for the human welfare, the justice and the human rights of all. In fact all religious have these concepts, but they don't care about these when issues come. This kind of common search and self-criticism only can bring about the harmony in relation to the issues regarding religious action-guides and legal action-guide.

This self-criticism is seen in the outlook of Raja Ram Mohun Roy, Gandhiji, Radhakrishnan, M.M. Thomas and other enlightened people from all religious communities. Two examples can be said on this context. If we take literally without consulting concept of "love your enemies", the actions that are done in the Old Testament (conquerring the enemies) can become a fundamental attitude in the present situation. In the case of *Gita* also this can happen. The modern Hindu scholars interpreted *Gita* as an inner conflict between evil and good. This is found in the comment of P.M. Thomas, "The delusion of Arjuna in the battlefield is very real and it is symbolic of the spiritual problems of all men" (P.M. Thomas, *20th century interpretations of Bhavagat Gita: Tilak, Gandhi and Aurobindo*, Bangalore: CISRS, 1987, p. 62). But it can cause religious riots and other fanatic attitudes if it is interpreted as the wicked and righteous. In the context of religious pluralism, for the fundamentalists the wicked will be none other than the people from the other religious community. According to P.M. Thomas, For Gandhiji, the great battle between Kauravas and Pandavas is the symbolic representation of the human heart (*Ibid.*, p. 92). He also believed that the central teaching of *Gita* is *Ahimsa*.

## Conclusion

The world is undergoing drastic changes because of modernization. But on the other hand there is severe threat from religious fundamentalism. The rigidity of religious communities are leading to so many competing claims and disputes. Here the role of a legal action-guide is crucial. In this context, it is necessary to have a rethinking from religious communities and law to decide on the criteria by which we can come to some solutions. This is a serious concern of ethics which is so much concerned about the harmony and integrity of the society. In order to form a criteria to decide the content of the legal action-guide and also the religious action-guides, a self-criticism is essential so also the elements of love, justice, human rights, and equality which are the essence of all religions so also the secular realm.

# 7
# Ekklesia as Community of Communities

"Ekklesia" in Greek is a secular term which denote the assembly of people with a purpose. They are gathered to get instruction or to make a public opinion related to the life of the people. It is a democratic assembly in the Graeco-Roman world. People are gathered in Courts and places as part of participatory decision-making. It has to be remembered that there was no or less participation of women. It shows the patriarchal nature of the assembly. In the Biblical context, 'ecclesia' (Ekklesia) is the septuagint translation of the Hebrew word 'Qohal' which refers to the congregation of Israel or the people of God.

The English word 'Church' is derived from the old English term 'Kirke' and that must have come from the Greek ideas such as 'Kyriake doma' or 'Kyriake oikia', which refers to the structure of the building (Lord's house). It is a gathering of people or a house. Ekklesia is an inclusive community of women and men. It should be also just community of women and men. In the *Old Testament* (Bible) the community is a covenant community, and a liberative community which affirms justice. The community of Yahweh was commanded to have love towards the powerless. The people of God are asked to have justice and concern towards the powerless. The instruction is given to regard the marginated like widows, orphans, slaves, fugitives, poor and the other victimized. The Old Testament was against the feudalism, and the prophets were challenging the oppressive structures that victimize the poor. It looks forward an egalitarian society where the identity, dignity and rights of the poor are upheld. The community of God's people are demanded to have a dialogical relationship with their neighbours. It is also urged to show compassion as God is compassionate to the poor. A proper social, economic and political relationship among the members is important to have a ecclesia of equals. The righteousness, justice and equity should prevail in the community of God's people. The concept of John Ruskin, 'one for all, and all for one' is having significant implication for the community of God's people. The concept of Jubilee and Shalom (peace) is meant for earning, sharing and liberation. It is to safeguard the interest of the poor. It is to emancipate the slaves. It is to share the land to the landless. It is to empower the disempowered.

*The New Testament* is focusing on the Kingdom of God and Kingdom community. Jesus movement did uphold the Kingdom values. It was a community of Subalterns. This community was a 'new creation' and new humanity. This community integrates the Jews and non-Jews. It is an inclusive community of the poor, sick and marginalized. It was a community of women and men. It was a healing, restoring and liberating community. That community was messianic and had prophetic consciousness as it upheld the spirituality of combat. Jesus movement was socialistic and it stood for radical transformation of the society which was oppressive and violent to the powerless. It was a community of the discipleship of equals.

Today, the 'ekklesia' has a wider discussion as it is a movement of different groups of people with their religious and ideological identities. In the social movements there is an integration and participation of people from different social, economic, political and religious backgrounds for a definite cause and purpose. The Narmada Valley Andolan, Chipko movement, the *dalit*, tribal and women movements are of this sort struggling to achieve a particular goal. They struggle against the injustices and human right violations. The transgenders, the sex workers and the migrants have their 'ekklesia'. They form as community to struggle for their rights. In Chengara (Kerala), the marginalized people have occupied the land as they protest the unjust structure which did not provide a space for them to live. They uphold the issues like right to land, right to have meaningful survival and the right to identity and dignity. The National Alliance of People's Movements (NAPM) is organizing different movements for the cause of justice, rights and dignity.

The civil society is now very conscious of the injustices and corruption. Anna Hazare's, 'India against corruption' is an example for this. People from all walks of life gather together to stand for a cause. The electronic devices are used to communicate the views. The cyber space is used also to build communities. It is cyber ekklesia or cyber communities through the websites, the facebook, Twitter and by blogs. People are brought together with a purpose. The virtual space is used as a platform to communicate and to gather for the common causes.

The 'ekklesia' has to be a responsible community which should uphold the poor and their concerns. The church and the larger ekklesia has to involve in the act of emancipation and empowerment of the poor. It should liberate the people from the dehumanizing situations. church should also come out the comfort zone to identify with the marginalized. It should be an open community to integrate the *dalits*, tribes, victimized women and other alienated people and it should work for their liberation. Faith and Praxis should play a vital role for this task. Ekklesia should transcend all forms of discriminations and disparities in order to be a community of peace with justice. Kingdom of God and its values have to be upheld as the socialistic vision has to be realized.

# 8

# Faith and Praxis

## Jesus, the Champion of Humanization

Our faith has to be expressed in praxis, so the faith and praxis should go together. Our faith, should not be dogmatic alone, but also pragmatic in nature. In Bonhoefferian understanding our faith should come out of the shells, and in the perspective of Gutierrez, faith has to come out of the shelf, that we should not keep the faith only in a dogmatic sense, but also in a praxiological sense.

The act of humanization is a dynamic exercise of praxis. Jesus is a champion of praxis as he humanized the structures of community.

### Jesus and His Message

Faith and praxis are integral to humanization in Jesus' understanding. The spiritual regeneration and the social transformation are integrated in Jesus' view. His messages are centred on repentance and the kingdom of God (MK 1:15). He challenged the people to change their ways, attitudes and perspectives (Mt. chapters 5-7). The Sermon on the Mount was a challenge against the Jewish legalism and superfluous spirituality. Jesus' messages urge the people to come to the understanding of faith which involves praxis. Jesus was leading the people to the essence of faith and the inner meaning of Torah (Jewish law). In the parable of the Good Samaritan also Jesus was scornful of the legalistic attitude of the Jews which denies the praxiological dimension of faith (L.K. 10:25 ff), and appreciated the faith of the Samaritan who put the faith into practice. The action is an important aspect of our faith. The social concern is the essential expression of our faith. Jesus' message was always leading to action (praxis). One of His dynamic message was the Nazareth Manifesto (LK. 4:16-21) in which he looked forward the transformation where faith and praxis integrate.

## The Dynamic Expression of Faith in Praxis

Jesus was not mere a preacher. He involved in the issues of the people in order to resolve them. He was always having solidarity with the least, lost and the last. The poor is central to Jesus' concern. As it is found in the Nazareth Manifesto, Jesus was working for the humanization of people and structures.

Jesus was actively involved in the liberation of the marginalized people as He challenged the structures of dehumanization. He identified with the issues of the poor, victimized women, the outcastes and the diseased. He moved with the powerless to empower them. He had a preferential option for the subalterns.

Jesus did question the dehumanizing factors which hinder to put faith into practice. He criticized the Pharisees who were the custodians of a peripheral faith and spirituality. The subbatical laws were challenged as they are reduced to be inhuman. The sabbatical laws were interpreted in such a way that the praxis was rejected. The life-affirming activities of Jesus were rejected by the religious leader of the time. His humanizing acts were also a threat to political leaders. So the unholy nexus between Jewish religious leaders and the Roman political leaders who were the mafia of the time tried to crucify Jesus in order to avoid his threat.

Jesus involved in the humanizing activity by healing the sick on the Sabbath day (John 5), listened to the cry of the Syro-Phoenician woman (Mt. 15:21), building a relationship with the so called outcastes such as publicans (Lk. 15:1-2, Lk. 19:1 ff) and

Samaritan women (John 4). He raised the dead, healed the sick and fed the hungry. He also brought a radical challenge by cleansing the temple which became the symbol of corrupt practices. Jesus was never intimidated to challenge evil (Mt. 21:12-13). The elements such as counter-culture, spirit of deconstruction, de-colonialism and de-legitimation are found in Jesus as he was criticizing the dominant evil local and imperial power structures.

## Faith and Praxis: The Implications of Humanization for Today

If we analyze the contextual issues of India today, the poverty is at the increase. It is found that over 250 million men, women and children go to bed hungry every night. Six out of every seven women are illiterate in the Indian context. Many women are victimized as they are harassed, raped and killed. They are objectified and sexually assaulted. The patriarchal society does deny their privileges. The condition of the *dalits*, tribes and other marginated groups are not better. Their identity, dignity and rights are denied. The rights of the minorities are also not protected in the Indian context.

The increase in the number of slums is the sure sign of increase in the marginated people. The slum dwellers are living in most unhealthy and unhygienic conditions. The income generating resources are in the hands of the minority rich and they control the social economic, political and religious structures. Exploitation and oppressions are a common scene in India. Corruption has become a way of life in the Indian situation. The United Nations development programme estimates that India's GDP (Gross Domestic Product) growth is cut by a quarter of what is possible because of corruption. The negative effect of globalization, the ecological problems like global warming, global climatic change, water scarcity, and the unemployment makes the life of the people difficult. There are also severe issues like terrorism and ethnic conflict.

It is important to respond to the unjust and dehumanizing structures to form an egalitarian society. Jesus was trying to build up a new community in line with values of the kingdom of God. The prophetic mission of Jesus was a challenge to all oppressive forces and the dehumanizing elements. As Jesus was never compromised with the inhuman elements, the Christian community has to involve in the act of humanization as God is humanizing, that is in Paul Lehmann's view, God is keeping human life human.

According to M.M. Thomas, the humanization is integral to the Gospel. In his words, 'Christianity will struggle for humanization best if we see the prophetic tradition as integral to the gospel of Christ (*Salvation and Humanization*, Madras, C.L.S., 1971, p. 34). He also states that "the mission of salvation and the task of humanization are integrally related to each other, even if they cannot be considered identical" (*Ibid*., p. 8). Christ is understood, by him, as the source and the foundation of true humanization. In the perspective of M.M. Thomas, faith and praxis are integrally related and it has to humanize.

In the epistle of James, a description of the relationship between faith and praxis is found. It is written, "What good is it, my brothers or sisters, if you say you have faith but do not have works? Can faith save you? If a brother and sister is naked and lacks daily food, and one of you says to them, "Go in peace, keep warm and eat your fill," and yet do not supply their body needs, what is the good of that? So faith by itself, if it has no works, is dead" (James. 2:14-17). Praxis is understood as the inseparable aspect of faith. Apostle James again comes to the conclusion that, "for just as the body without the spirit is dead, so faith without works in also dead" (James 2:26).

As a response to the challenges the Indian people faces, Fr. Sebastian Kappen states, "the gospel can also help distinguish between genuine spurious responses to the divine will revealed in history. Jesus' teaching that where the divine presents itself in time and space the hungry are filled, the thirst for justice is quenched and all humans made free for love and universal communion shows that the humanization of the world is the only sure index of divinization" (*Liberation Theology and Marxism,* Puntamba: Asha Kendra, 1986, p. 5). The praxis or the humanization is an indispensable factor in the Indian context and the world at large as God himself through Jesus Christ intensively involved in the humanizing process to redeem everyone, especially the subalterns from the clutches of oppression.

## Conclusion

The mission that Jesus introduced is a humanizing mission as M.M. Thomas stated salvation includes humanization. God's mission is salvific and it is holistic in nature. The responsibility today is to liberate the people from the clutches of evil which is personal and structural in form. The mission of the Christian community is to build up a humane community which upholds love, justice and peace. Praxiological dimension of Christian faith should be central to our life and mission. Our faith has to inspire us to do praxis so that we may involve in the task of alleviation of poverty, relief and rehabilitation, disaster management, development programmes and also to liberate the Subalterns from their plight.

# 9
# The Struggles of the Migrants

It is an era of migration as migration has become inevitable in search of employment, better prospects or to find a place (piece of land) for shelter. It is an international phenomena. There is permanent and temporary migrations. Those who go for employment may have temporary migration, as they come back after their tenure. Some people may settle there also as they find prospects there. Economic stability is a main concern in migration. So many people from Third World are migrating to United States and other European countries for employment and permanent settlement. Many people are temporarily migrating to Gulf countries in search of employment. There are migrants in the form of refugees in the context of war, disasters and other disturbances.

Migration from rural areas to urban setting is also very common in Indian context. This is because there is more facilities (water, transportation, telecommunication etc.) and employment opportunities in cities. There is also more freedom and dignity for women and other subaltern groups (e.g. *dalits* and tribes) in cities as the values are more secularized and context is heterogenous. When there is violence because of religious fundamentalism, caste war or terrorism, people migrate to other places for safety and security. There is migration in the form of invasion. Their purpose is to conquer and subjugate and settle there. The Aryans invaded India and settled here. There was migration for the survival from Mangolia, China, Tibet, Burma and Bangladesh to India. The Zorastrians or Parsees had migrated to India as the fundamentalist groups in Iran had attacked them. They sought refuge in India. There was migration from Persia and Israel (Jews) to India. Some people migrate also for the purpose of business. There is also forced migration as the people are evacuated in the name of development. The inhabitants are forcefully evacuated from Narmada valley for the sake of 'development' is an example. When there is extreme poverty in villages, the people also migrate as families in search for employment and food. Temporary or permanent migrations are also taking place when there is natural disasters or ecological problems. It is predicted that because of global climatic change there may be a migration of many people to other countries and place, as there is possibility of submerging of some places. This climatic change creates an issue of land.

It is clear that migration are of different kinds: it can be in search for: (1) food, (2) employment, (3) acquiring land-invasion, (4) security, (5) survival, (6) dignified life, (6) facilities and opportunities, (7) business, (8) a piece of land (for shelter). There is two types of migration-temporary and permanent. According to Dr. G.K. Karant (Professor of Sociology, University of Bangalore) migrant is one who is not local. In his view, modern condition is that we are new nomads. He also argues that migrant is usually staying permanently. Migrants also try to recreate their culture in the new situation. Migrants can, in his view, become villains as they use violence against locals. Migrants, he states, have killed the Red Indians of United States. Among the migrants, according to him, there can be cultural independence or cultural assimilation.

The migration can be in local level (one locality to another), district level (one district to another), state level (one state to another) or national level (one country to another). Migration can be monocultural (same culture) or cross-cultural in character. If we analyse the story of every person and family, everyone is a nomad or migrant. This migration is a continuous process, and it happens all through the countries in all centuries.

There is legal and illegal migrations. Illegal migrants do not keep the rules and regulations. Some countries promote the migration (e.g. Canada, New Zealand etc.) as they have less population. The cosmopolitan cities like Bombay and Bangalore constitute more migrants from Kerala, Thailand, Andhra Pradesh and other Indian States. The employment and business are some of their major concerns. It is also to be noted that there is also the growing menace of 'sons of soil theory'. Recently, there is a great migration of workers from West Bengal, Odisha and Bihar to the state of Kerala. There is unrest in Indian States like Odisha, North East and West Bengal because of migration from other states and from Bangladesh.

Migration is understood as a movement of people from their place of settlement or origin to another distant place. We will find migrants among domestic workers, construction workers and slum-dwellers. The poor, children and the men and women are among the migrants. There are *dalits* and tribes among them. According to Census Survey of India, Internal migration are intra-state and inter-state in nature (Augustine Kanjamala, "social analysis of migration in India", *Migration and Mission in India,* edited L. Stanislaus and Jose Joseph, Delhi: Isvani Kendra/ISPCK, 2007 p. 2). E.G. Ravenstein's theory of migration states that 'migration increases in volume as industries and commerce develop and transport improves'. The major cause of migration for him is economic. In the 'push and pull theory' of Evert Lee, migration means 'pushes' from the areas of origin and 'pulls' to areas of destination. In the view of Michael Todaro, potential migrants would consider the various market opportunities available to them as between the rural and urban sectors and choose one which maximizes their expected gain from migration. In the understanding of Marxian School, migration is the creation of capitalistic productive sector. Industrialization and profit accumulation created a poor surplus working class, which was forced to migrate to cities. In the post-modern theory, migration is now global. Migrants are immigrating from poor countries to rich countries. These theories are summarised by Augustine

Kanjamala (*Ibid.*, pp. 3-5). The personal, social, economic, religious, cultural and political reasons are found in the question of migration.

The migrants are facing so many issues such as identity crises, alienation, exploitation, oppression and insecurity. The 'sons of soil' movement also creates a threatening situation for migrants. Those migrants who found good employment or prosperity in business will root well in the new situation. But those who did not have economic stability have to live in poverty or to find refuge in slums. For the locals, the migrants can create problem in the sharing of resources. The locals may think that their employment opportunities may be lost, and they can also create space problem. Migrants may be also considered as exploiters by the locals. They have to live in stress and strain and also in a situation of 'no recognition' as the locals may not accommodate them. Their identity, dignity and rights are, sometimes, questioned and rejected. They are also considered as outsiders. The lion's-share of the migrants are Subalterns as they are forced to live in most dehumanized situation. They are poor and also marginalized.

Migrants have to undergo social and psychological struggles. Sometimes they may not get acceptance and support from the locals. The exclusive attitude of the locals can create a feeling of alienation for the migrants. The urban population is at the increase because of migration to cities which creates issue of space, employment, and lack of basic facilities.

It is important to have a creative response to migrants. Migrants are finding a new destination for survival. It is to be acknowledged that everyone is a migrant, so the migrants' identity, dignity and rights are to be recognized. Migration is an inevitable phenomenon as no one can confine to local situation as the people find better prospects if they move to different situations. Migrants have to be sensitive to identify with the situation and try to avoid creating any conflict. The migrants also have to be open minded and adjust with the new situation and relate with the local people. This is important to avoid any suspicion on the migrant. The society has to support the migrants in order to be rooted in the new situation. So that they may overcome the strains and alienation. The church has a missional responsibility to undergird the migrants, as they look forward the love, care and support. An inclusive approach is essential to uphold the migrants.

Bible is holding an inclusive approach to the migrants. They are sojourners, fugitives or aliens. Bible does not permit to oppress the alien or stranger, who is a migrant (Exodus 22:21, 23:9). The Israelites were also migrants (strangers), so they are not supposed to oppress them. God always safeguard the migrant. Love and Justice is due to the migrants as God loves the Sojourners (Deuteronomy 10:18, 19). The Hebrews were referred by God as migrants (Lev. 25:23). God is the protector and liberator of migrants (Lev. 25:38). As the alienated people, God sides the migrants. Abraham and the Hebrews were migrants and God promised them a space to settle. These migrants (Hebrews) were not accepted by the surrounding peoples, but God was acting as their liberator. God always has solidarity with the people who undergo struggles and suffering. Jesus was also concerned of the migrants. He was compassionate to the cause of the centurion and even the cananite woman and other Jewish and non-jewish poor and marginalized (Luke 7:1-10, Mark. 7:24-30, Lk. 7:11-17). Bible has recognized the identity, dignity and rights of migrants. Jesus was also a migrant to earth from heaven (Jn 1:14; Phili 2:6-8). He incarnated into the earth as a migrant. Justice and equality are to be upheld as we deal with the issues of the migrants. They are also created in God's image (Gen. 1:27, 28). The UN declaration of Human Rights and also the Constitution of India have protected the rights of the migrants (Universal Declaration of Human Rights Article (1) states that all human beings are born free and equal in dignity and rights. They are endowed with reason and conscience and should act towards one another in a spirit of 'brotherhood'. Article (6) states, "Everyone has the rights to recognition everywhere as a person before the law". The Constitution of India, Article 19(e) states, 'all citizens shall have the right to move freely and to reside and settle in any part of the territory of India. The migrants have their identity and rights and they are not supposed to be mis-treated.

There are rich and poor migrants, and they undergo so many struggles. But here more concern is needed for the migrants who are poor and marginalized as they are undergoing extreme forms of alienation and oppression. They even have to find shelter in slums and to live in extreme poverty. The government, the society, the Church and other voluntary organizations have to pay attention to the struggles of the migrants and help them to be liberated from the suffering and oppression.

# 10
# Response to Issues of Transgenders

One of the very marginated groups is the transgenders. They are undergoing severe identity crisis, alienation and deprivation. The society and the Government authorities have failed to recognize their issues. Their identity, dignity and rights are denied by them. They have to stay away from the mainstream of the society as they are not recognized. They are a Subaltern group who have to confine to their own community or elsewhere. In Indian context, most of the transgenders involve in domestic work, begging and sex work.

## Transgender

A person's sex is determined at birth as male or female or transgender. The transgender can be referred also as inter-sexual, heterosexual, bi-sexual, pan sexual, polysexual or asexual. They are also identified as 'third gender'. There are also terms like 'eunuch,' 'agender' and 'genderqueer' to refer them. In the Indian context, the words like '*Hijra*' (*Hijada*), '*Sikhandi*,' '*Aravanis*' are used to refer them. Christine Jorgensen (in 1979) rejected the word 'transexual' and supported the term 'transgender' as she argued that gender is nothing to do with sex but with identity. The concept of a 'transgender community' was formed in 1984. In India, we have a transgender community called 'Sangama' (in Bangalore), which was established in 1999.

In biology, transexuality is a sexual disorder. According to Elaine Storkey, 'the disorder', 'S alpha-reductese deficiency' (an enzyme deficiency)—results in genetic males being born with genitalia of female appearance' (*Men and Women—Created or Constructed,* Secunderabad: OM Authentic, 2001, p. 23). She continued to say, "the counter disorder in women-cogenital adrenal hyperplasia—is genetically recessive condition that leads to vinilisation of females, i.e. genetically female children are born with masculinised genitalia with again a resultant confusion of identity" (*Ibid.*, p. 23).

Transgenders can be grouped into two transmen (men trapped in women body) and transwomen (women trapped in men body). Transgenders are referred as omnigenders, Ladyboy and Androgyne. They try to show the feminine feelings and identify with women (in their dress and behaviour). The Gender-queer is explained as gender experience that do not fit into binary concepts, and refers to a combination of gender identities and sexual orientations. The gender presentation sometimes appear as male, and sometimes female. It shows non-conformity. Androgyne is not fitting to any typical gender roles. It is stated "Androgynes may identify as beyond gender, between genders, moving across genders, entirely genderless, or any or all of these exhibiting a variety of male, female, and other characteristics. Androgyne identities include pangender, ambigender, non-gender, agender, genderfluid or intergender. Androgyny can be either physical or psychological, and it does not depend on birth sex" (Websters' Medical Dictionary).

We have now found the emergence of the LGBT (Lesbian, Gay, Bi-Sexual, Transgender) community which affirm their sexual orientations and identity. It has developed as a sub-culture. In order to have the protection of rights the transgender community allay with the movement of lesbians, gay and bi-sexuals.

The *Hijras* or *Hijadas* are also called *Jagappa* or *Aravani* (*Aruvani*). They are the eunuchs. *Hijras* are organized themselves and live in communities under a *guru*. The *Hijras* are psychologically males who have famine gender identity and adopts feminine gender roles and women's clothing. The *Jogappas* are like born male, appear in *sarees*.

The word '*Hijra*' is derived from the Arabic root '*hjr*' which means 'leaving one's tribe'. The similar aspect is found in English 'eunuch' or 'Hermaphrodite' which refers to persons who have irregularity of the male genitalia. *Hijras* are found on streets, trains and other public places demanding money from people. The Indian story is that when Arjuna, Indra's son, went to heaven, Urvasi had an attraction on him. Arjuna rejected the plea of Urvasi as she was wife of Indra, his father. But Urvasi cursed him to be a transgender.

The word '*kothi*' is also used to refer the transgenders in India. They are distinguished from *Hijras*. They are considered as feminine men or boys who take a feminine role in sex with men. It is like feeling as women, but born as man.

## The Life and Struggle of Transgenders

The transgenders are facing discrimination from parents, friends, classmates and society. When these children are born, and the 'mother' (who is a *guru* or leader of transgender community) is watching the movements of the children as they are growing. Usually as they face severe alienation and ill-treatment, they run away from home, and here 'mother' appears as a rescuer.

The identity, dignity and rights of the trasngenders are denied. Usually they have no identity cards or ration cards. Their citizenship is ignored, especially in the Indian context. Getting job is also not easy for them, so most of them involve in begging and sex work. They are disturbed by *Gundas*, policemen and others in order to have sexual exploitation and to grab money from them. They are facing violence from the society. They are also victims of systemic violence. They are denied of legal rights and social justice. Most of the *Hijras* are living at the margins of the society with very low status. They are the marginalized or subaltern. Employment opportunities are also very less to *Hijras*.

The *Hijra* Sex workers face brutal violence in public spaces, police stations and prisons.

The Governments of India and Pakistan have recognized *Hijras* as 'third sex' and granted them basic rights of every citizen. They are given the option to identify as eunuch ("E") in passport and other documents. There were instances in which the right to vote and candidature are denied in general elections.

The transgenders formed their own communities in several places and they have their own organizations. It so happens that their life is not secure even in the transgender community. When they are not able to bring money, their status is low and life becomes miserable. When they become old or seriously sick, their condition will be pathetic. Since majority are involved in sex work, they have the risk of venereal diseases and HIV/AIDS.

The public life of a transgender is also very tragic. There is only a discriminative attitude towards a transgender. They are not able to identify with the other members of the audience in the public meetings. They also may face the problem, where to sit? To sit with men or women is the issue they face. How they introduce themselves is another problem. Whenever they come to the main stream they face acute identity problem. The attitude of the society to a transgender is dehumanizing.

**Responses**

The transgenders should be accepted without any reservations by the society. They are also human beings with identity, dignity and rights. Their right of citizenship, ration card, voter identity card and the such should be upheld. The parents, family members and the society should recognize them. They also have the right to education, health care and employment. Their active participation in the main stream of the society has to be promoted. The different kinds of oppressions and exploitations and violence against their humanhood has to be questioned. It is important to develop a just community or an inclusive community where the transgenders should have meaningful participation.

Transgenders are a marginalized group who are also created in the image of God (Gen. 1:27, 28). God listens and acts on the cry of any marginalized group. No one can deny justice to the transgenders (Lk. 4:16-21). The freedom and liberation are envisioned for the transgenders also.

They are an oppressed humanity who are to be loved, cared and supported. The society should shed their inhuman attitude towards the transgenders. God always undergird the people who are weak and rejected. It is our responsibility to evolve a humane attitude towards the transgenders They are to be dealt with love and humanness as they are physically and psychologically tortured. Don't consider them as a curse which is a traditional attitude towards them, but provide every possibilities for them to come up and explore their creativity for the good of the whole society. It should also be considered that they have the right to be an integral part of the religious communities and rites. Their status, roles and positions have to be recognized in the society.

# 11

# Mission in the Context of Globalization

The world is globalized as there is social, economic, political, religious and cultural factors involved in them. It looks for the accessibility to everywhere. The socio-economic dimension is related to liberalization. In the political context there is neo-colonialism, and in religious context there is an export and import of different religious practices and movements. In the cultural context, the western music, cinemas, entertainments and technologies are transported to the Eastern world by the West.

## I. The Context of Globalization

Globalization is a unification process by which every aspect of life can be made related. It is an ideology which is used by the western countries to impose their values to the other countries. It is neo-colonial in nature. It is a free-market economy or *laizzes faire*. It is a cheap labour policy of western countries that they use the resources of the east to make products and sell them to all countries in international prices. They calculate the price based on the European countries. They may make a shirt which only costs Rs. 75 but they sell it for Rs. 1500 (in India and in US and other European countries). There are exploitative commercial policies involved in Globalization. There is competition and power struggle in the market, where the economically and politically powerful will win. It also leads to a marginalization. Because of marginalization there is 'Globalization of Poverty' as

Michel Chassudosky argues. The patent laws and the genetically modified or terminated seeds are to be understood in the light of the negative effects of globalization.

Globalization also challenges what is native or local and traditional. The values of traditional economy, social life, and the culture are being questioned. The traditional way of life, perspectives, knowledge, skills, music, medicines, food, religiosity, communication are undergoing challenges. There is, now, a heavy dependence on what is western. The cyber space is also used very much in this context. The information technologies and electronic media (TV, computer, internet facilities, and mobile phones) are also playing vital role in globalization. The cyber space is also part and parcel of the post-modern society. 'You-tube', 'Facebook', blogs and the websites are also part of the virtual/cyber space. They can be used creatively and improperly as there is positive and negative use of these devices.

According to Michel Amaladoss, cultural globalization seeks to spread the 'gospel' of modern culture as a necessary underpinning of economic and political globalization. A materialistic outlook on life and reality, a spirit of individualism and competition, an attitude of consumerism, an approach of autonomy in the name of science from ethical and religious control, profit-oriented commercial activity are some of the characteristics of this culture. There is an ideal of unity as uniformity and intolerance of pluralism" ("Introduction," *Globalization and its victims as seen by its victims,* edited by Michel Amaladoss, New Delhi: ISPCK, 1999, p. vii). Globalization looks for universalism and centralization. According to Michel Amaladoss, "there is a right of Globalization that respects pluralism and identity but promotes convergence and communication, making proper use of the facilities of science, technology and the media" (*Ibid.*, p. xi). It is important to tackle the negative effects of globalization which promotes the reckless development that do not consider the ecology, the poor, and the right of the people who are subalterns (e.g. tribes and *dalits*).

In negative effect of globalization, Walter Fernandes identifies the issues like a monopolization of natural resources, homogenization of culture, internationalization of capital and trade, technological transformation resulting in employment and livelihood opportunities, particularly to the poor, and the withdrawal or drastic reduction of subsidies required by the poor ("Globalization, liberalization and the victims of colonialism", *Globalization and its victims as seen by its victims* edited by Michel Amaladoss, p. iii).

According to Leon Diouf, there are factors like strong bases of domination that is the consequence of enlightenment and the Western hegemony that was a contribution of Christian Europe (developed a hierarchy or pyramid where God is at the top, then Kings and nobles, then people, and finally plants, animals and material objects) which also find its roots for globalization ("Globalization and its cultural underpinnings" *Globalization and its victims as seen by its victims,* edited by Michel Amaladoss, pp. 109-110). The spirit of competition and domination that leads to exploitation and oppression.

## II. The Influence of Globalization

It is to be noted that there a certain positive influence of Globalization, which is also related to the modernization.

It is a cyber age where cyber space is used for communication. The global media, the global communication and the electronic devices are a boon, if they are responsibly used. The development of the information technology is useful for the people. So the society today is understood as 'Knowledge society' or 'Information society'. We are now part and parcel of 'information highway'. It is also to be noted that there devices are also used by the Western countries for cultural invasion. It is also used as a means to transport the sex elements and wrong value systems. Religious fundamentalists, terrorists and anti-social elements are using their technologies to spread provocative messages which can misguide the people.

The misinformation and the spreading of what is unethical through these communication devices can spoil the youths and others. These facilities can be used for bringing programmes which can conscientize the society and inculcate a proper value system. As already stated, the consumerism, profit-orientation, competition and bringing damage to native culture and exploitation of indigenous resources are the negative influence of the neo-liberal policies.

Felix Wilfred was critical of globalization as a way of life and attitude. He describes the change of attitude as follows "the basic attitude of life is short through a crass pragmatism centred on money, consumer-goods, career, etc. It is interesting for example, to observe how today the students in institutes of higher education are gripped by another set of values than the political and social ideas of earlier times. The generation of students in late 1960s and 1970s fought vigorously for social issues and went on *dharnas*, protests and fasts. This student culture is replaced today by pragmatic considerations of career advancement, competition and search for money-making avenues" (*Asian Dreams and Christian hope at the dawn of the millennium,* Delhi: ISPCK, 2000, p. 13.). He again states "the new attitudes, values and way of life unleashed by globalization and liberalization are dramatically opposed to the attitudes, values required for the cause of liberation of those at the periphery" (*Ibid.*, p. 14).

Felix Wilfred also questions the homogenizing of globalization. He argues, "No nation, no people, no country can make progress on the basis of borrowed identity. Globalization is a process of losing our identity in its rich diversity. Therefore, we need to find ways and means to strengthen the local, the regional, and the contextual. True universality has meaning only among peoples, groups who are well-rooted in their cultures and traditions" (*Ibid.*, p. 16).

The negative effects include 'the globalization of poverty' as the poor have no accessibility to the resources and they are chased away from their habitat in the name of development, and they are also used for cheap labour. In globalization, the powerful can achieve their exploitative ends. The exploitation of resources and the consequent ecological degradation is another major threat to humanity, which is contributed by globalization. The reckless tapping of minerals, coal, and other resources and also deforestation in the name of development also affects the life of the indigenous peoples and the biodiversity and it leads to the depletion of resource. According to Walter Fernandes, "To understand its consequences, one should remember that in India at least 30 million persons have been displaced by development project since 1951" ("Globalization, Liberalization and the victims of colonialism", *Globalization and its victims as seen by its victims,* edited by Michel Amaladoss, p. 9). The globalization also leads to marginalization of women, states Walter Fernandes (*Ibid.*, p. 17). The women confront issues like poverty, gender discrimination, unemployment, malnutrition and become victims of environmental degradation (*Ibid.*, pp. 18-19). The *dalit* and tribal women are mostly affected than the dominant women.

Globalization is not concerned of the values that undergird the poor or to develop a community which is based on justice, dignity and rights. It is not concerned of ethics. Globalized culture is meant as Western and it uproots the native culture and values. Western values are based on, as globalization upholds, capitalism, consumerism, individualism, legitimized immoral sexual practices and entertainments and these are transported to Asia and other Third World countries. According to Francis Jayapathy, "It is only when persons belonging to different cultures meet in a climate of acceptance and respect for the other cultures, communicate to each other in a spirit of dialogue which affirms the multiplicity of worldviews and their validity as worldview, could one expect to see the positive and healthy development of whatever might emerge as a global culture" ["I buy, therefore, I exist", *Jeevadhara*, vol. xxv, No. 145 (January, 1995), p. 11].

Globalization is an exploitative consumeristic profit-oriented, objectifying, destructive and domineering dogma which is used as an ideology to manipulate the other, especially the powerless and poor. It is pro-rich and pro-elitistic. As an integral part of modernism, globalization and its values are not concerned of poor, women, *dalits*, tribes, fisherfolk, other indigenous groups, slum-dwellers, the people with disabilities and other victimized groups. Globalization values the competent, the powerful and the dominant. It never values the nature or creation, as it sees the nature as a resource to be exploited for making money. It also transports music, electronic devices, entertainment programmes and behavioural patterns which can cater to the interests of the rich and dominant. It is to be noted that the Western elites and Third World elites are sharing a common culture, as Third World elites imitate the West. The positive social and religious values of the Third World countries are being eroded as the effect of globalization. It is a capital intensive money-oriented and trade related ideology which cannot do justice to humanity. It has no human face and it is an oppressive ideology which dehumanizes the powerless people.

Globalization is rooted in commerce and trade, and it is leading the people to the comfort zone of luxury, consumption or consumerism. It is also based on privatization and accumulation of wealth and property by few. The powerful like investors, technocrats and bureaucrats are trying to draw a huge amount of money and it is used for luxurious life and this vested interest is also contributing to global economic recess. In globalization, money, land, and other income-generating resources are centred around the wealthy and powerful. It is a systemic violence which dehumanizes the powerless. The value of human beings in globalization is based only on the purchasing capacity of the persons.

## III. The Challenge of Christian Mission to Globalization

What should be a Christian response to globalization from the missional perspective? The Christian approach has to be dynamic, concrete, contextual, creative and relevant. There are several issues to be tackled in the context of globalization.

### *1. Tackling the Issue of Poverty*

Around 200 crore people are undergoing poverty. In India itself more than 50 per cent of people are in poverty. They are facing issue like unemployment, malnutrition, lack of food and water, no shelter, and no proper sanitation facilities. Globalization marginalizes people, especially the powerless. The rural and urban poor are struggling to survive, as there is no possibility for a dignified existence. Most of them are also landless.

What is our missional response to the poor? Earth has resources to meet the needs of all its inhabitants, if the resources are responsibly used and equitably distributed. Our public distribution system is also not functioning properly. The rich and powerful are grabbing the privileges of the poor. Cheap labour policy of globalization and the growing unemployment are becoming the severe social problems which can be tackled only by following a socialist pattern of social structure which can cater to the needs of all people. The *dalits* are in extreme poverty and most of them are shelterless and unemployed. The tribal hamlets in many parts of India are without proper electricity, water supply, food, and sanitation. Many members of tribes are dying without food. They are affected by malnutrition.

It is very important to offer the dignified life to the victimized of globalization. Mere 'food security bill' is not an answer to tackle the issue of poverty and malnutrition. Employment is essential to buy food. Though tonnes of food items are spoiled in the godowns of Food Corporation of India and other private firms, and it is not distributing to the starving poor. Since commercialization, profiteering and individualism are the key factors of globalization, they have no mission to serve the poor. This has to be tackled by the organized struggles of the poor. It is also important to note that the poor women and children are doubly victimized of poverty and malnutrition than the poor men.

The unjust and exploitative structures are to be questioned to overcome the situation of poverty. It is an oppressive structure which contributes to poverty. Justice and human rights are denied to the poor. Our mission should be based on the Kingdom of God, which is based on justice and peace. *The Old Testament* prophets condemned the latifundialization (it is the accumulation of large amount of land by the powerful which form into estates. It becomes an oppressive and exploitative structure) and the consequent poverty. Bible supports poor, and it looks for an egalitarian society (Lev. 25). In the *New Testament*, Jesus was siding the poor and Jesus' movement was a threat to inhuman structures of feudalism and colonialism. The unjust structures are being questioned by Jesus as he had solidarity with the poor. Jesus' movement was the movement of the poor and powerless and it was the hope of the poor. Through feeding the hungry and challenging the unjust structures, he was tackling the problem of poverty. The New Testament also provides a model for sharing (in Greek 'koinonia' the resources in order to cater to the needs of the poor (Acts. 2:44-45; 4:32-35; 2 Cor. 8:1ff). The early Christian community was also closely following the ethics of Jesus' movement. It was upholding the values such as justice, peace, sharing and equality. It was a socialistic community. The Christian Church today has to follow this values in order to help the poor to overcome poverty.

### 2. Tackling the Issue of Illiteracy and Health Problems

Though there are many graduates in India, compared to any other countries in the world, the education of the poor, *dalit*, tribes and the poor woman is not hopeful. At least 35 per cent of the Indians are illiterate and the lion's share of this is the marginalized groups. The privatization and liberalized policies of globalization make the quality education inaccessible to the poor. Because of poverty, many of the poor children are either not going to school or they drop out from school as they go for work for their survival. Those who do not have money cannot go for good education. The professional studies are also accessible only to those who have sound economic position. Even mission schools, colleges and professional colleges are not concerned of the poor and other subaltern groups, as they are also focusing on acquiring money through high fees.

The health and hygiene is also a serious issue. The health facilities are provided to the urban rich and not the urban and rural poor. The liberalization and privatization have imposed the reduction of subsidies and concessions and free services which are availed by the poor and marginalized. The quality health facilities are only accessible to the rich. The mission hospitals are established in the cities focusing on the rich and their money. Now education and health facilities are commercialized and looking for profit. These became a lucrative business. The poor cannot, now, afford quality education and health facilities.

The deceptive and exploitative falconry of oppression of Globalization has to be challenged. The primary concern of the churches, the government authorities and also the voluntary organizations should make the educational and medical facilities to the poor accessible. The Christian institutions should have a proper missional focus so that the education and health of the poor can be given adequate attention and care. Education and health care are very costly all over the world, where the poor are denied of the rights. Their right to education and health is in crisis. Education and health care should have a human face to serve the humanity, especially the powerless. Education and health care became the privilege of the rich, and poor are undergoing severe struggle as they cannot afford the big amount of payment.

### *3. Tackling the Issue of the Exploitation and Oppression*

Globalization is neo-colonialism. It is an oppressive ideology. It affirms the view that only competent and powerful can meaningfully survive. It makes maximum effort to create dependence on the powerful countries, the elites and the dominant. It promotes cheap labour. It attempts to destroy the local or indigenous agriculture, industries and value systems and economy. It encourages rash use of technology without considering the environmental issue and people's life. It aims at exploiting the resources of the people for the benefit of the Western countries and the Eastern elites and investors. There is an unholy nexus between politicians, the western forces and eastern industrialists to exploit the resources cheaply and to share the maximum profit. The patent laws, the terminated seeds and huge investments in other countries are the instruments of exploitation for the advocates of globalization. The multinational companies became the vehicle of globalization. They exploit the metal ores, the minerals and other resources for their benefit. They also make the Third World their market by which they sell their electronic devices, medicines and food items to tap the money. Coca-cola, Pepsi-cola, Kentucky Fried Chicken (KFC) are the common items of the neo-colonial powers available in our country. It is an invasion as it challenges and destroys our traditional food items and habits. These companies are spending huge amount of money for advertisement in order to tempt the people to buy their products.

The multinational companies are exploiting the resources in the name of development and they are chasing the *dalits* and tribal people from their habitats. They are left as migrants and are forcefully evacuated with the help of the government machinery. The bio-diversity is also highly affected as there is deforestation. The force of globalization makes the life of the poor more miserable as they are already undergoing centuries long suffering of different kinds of oppressions.

The Christian mission has to challenge the forces of injustice and side with the victims of globalization, the exploited and oppressed, and work for their liberation. A 'spirituality of combat' is important to tackle this issue. The Christian community has to challenge the structural evil and work for the empowerment of the poor. Service to humanity is not merely charity, but it is something that is dealing with the life related issues of the poor and marginalized. Upholding the rights and redeem the people from the oppressive form and protecting the environment are very important Christian responsibilities. Our missional response should not be peripheral, but dynamic. It is very necessary to involve in the struggles of the poor for justice, as it is a missional response.

### *4. Tackling the Issue of the Misguiding Values*

Globalization is also importing Western value system through their art, dances, music and life style. Globalization is objectifying the women and the poor. Western value system is promoting free sex culture such as homosexuality, lesbianism, cohabitation and divorces. These are legitimized by them. The traditional music, dances and art are being challenged and what is Western is being recognized as 'valuable'. The traditional understanding of marriage and parenthood are also being questioned. Sex became an object of enjoyment and this notion has misguided the people which lead to moral laxity. The sexual violence over girls and women is the result of this misguided value system.

It is important to inculcate a strong sense of moral values to guide the people, especially the youth in the proper way. Our missional task is to conscientize the people with the proper value system. The Christian community has to challenge the immoral practices like irresponsible divorces, cohabitation, homosexual relationships, alcoholism, drug addiction, sexual violence, sex appealing and pleasure seeking art and music. We have to act as a moral guide to the people and conscientize the people with proper moral values. An organized effort of the Christian community is necessitated to challenge and to respond to the evils of globalization.

# 12

# The Golden Rule as a Paradigm for Doing Theology and Ethics in the Indian Context

Several suggestions might come to develop a paradigm for doing theology and ethics in the Indian context. The golden rule is found to be one of the viable paradigm for doing theology and ethics in the Indian context. 'Whatever you wish that men would do to you, do so to them' (Mk. 7:12; Lk. 6:31) is the golden rule. The golden rule can be a fitting paradigm in the Indian context.

## I. The Issues from the Indian Context

The Indian context is pluralistic. There is social, economic, political, religious pluralisms and a cultural diversity. The diverse value systems also exist in India.

In the area of social pluralism, the caste hierarchy is one of the major problems. The caste system promotes the dominance of the high caste, and it denounces the so-called low castes, who are known as *dalits*. The *dalits* are the oppressed, exploited and the marginated. They are the poor and suffering from unemployment, shelterless condition, insufficient food (they are going to bed without meal or with a square meal), malnutrition, inadequate educational or health facilities.

The *dalits* are living in the most subhuman living conditions. They are dehumanized and their experience is one of poverty and inferior status. Their dignity is not approved by the elites. The *dalits* are undergoing poverty, while rich are leading a very luxurious life. The economic pluralism is that the gulf between the rich and the poor is widening in a rapid pace. Forty per cent of the Indian masses are living below the poverty-line. There is, of course, an economic pluralism. The rich and the poor are the two main classes in India. It is important to note that the *dalits* and tribes belong to the lower class. They are the poorest among the poor as they are socially and economically deprived and politically voiceless. They are exploited and oppressed systematically by the dominant.

The poor in India are malnourished, illiterate/less literate, deprived of the adequate medical and educational facilities, unemployed and insecure. The tribes of India are also going through the same experience. The *dalit* and tribal women are sexually abused, tortured and even killed by the so called upper caste men. The women are, on the whole, indiscriminately ill-treated by the patriarchal system of India. While describing the condition of Indian women, Indu B. Nair states that, "The police, the protectors of law and order, wealth and property, use women who come into their hold, for sexual gratification. Being a complaint or witness is as dangerous as being a culprit." (Unmasking the faces of death-stories from the lives of Indian women", *Struggle Against Death,* edited by M.J., Joseph, Kottayam: Editorial Board of Study Programme, 1982, p. 67).

The varieties of religious experiences and the religious fundamentalism is another main aspect of the Indian context. The Hindu, Jain, Buddhist, Muslim, Parsi and the Christian are living in India with their particular faiths. Tolerance, *ahimsa* and harmony have been acclaimed as the ideals of Indian heritage. But today though India is known as a secular country, the religious fanaticism is emerging in a dangerous pace. Hindutva ideology and the politicizing of religion is creating disharmony in the Indian Society. The Hindutva ideology is fascist as it advocates for the annihilation of the non-Hindus. It will only help to develop hatred, disrespect and mistrust among the communities as against love and brotherhood.

The cultural diversity is another important phenomenon. There are diverse value systems existing in India. There are values which are to be upheld. At the same time, the inhuman and evil practices (e.g. *sati*, caste system, *devadasi* system etc.) also prevail in our land which is to be condemned. The systemic violence (e.g. violence against women, *dalits*, tribes and poor) is found very much in the Indian context.

The exploitation of the resources and the violence over the creation by the dominant groups is one of the severe problems which is to be curbed. The government also supports the violence in the form of deforestation and forceful evacuation of the tribes, who are the inhabitants in that area, in the name of development. A rash and irresponsible approach to creation should be condemned. Our environment is abused or manipulated by the dominant and powerful one for economic gains instead of undergirding the eco-system. The inhuman structure are torturing or ravaging the nature or creation. The ethos of today's society is capitalistic. The capitalistic forces interpret or conceive the life in economic terms which leads to selfishness, competition and accumulation of wealth. Protecting the nature, preserving the bio-diversity, the welfare of the people and upholding the dignity and rights of the marginated are not important concerns for capitalistic forces. They are after economic exploitation so also the exploitation over nature and not for the integrity of creation. When we do harm to the environment, we are doing harm to the whole humanity as they are to suffer the consequences of the ecological problems. The greenhouse effect, global warming, acid rains, water scarcity, air pollution, water pollution, soil pollution and the damage done to ozone layer and radiation are all consequences of irresponsible management of mankind to the environment.

## II. The Implications of the Golden Rule for Doing Theology and Ethics in the Indian Context

The Golden rule is an important tool to do theology and ethics in the present Indian global context. It stimulates us to relate ourselves responsible to the issues in the particular situations.

### *(a) The Essence of the Golden Rule*

The crux of the golden rule is altruistic. It indicates that others are important as we are. We should have care and concern for others, for others need our love, care and support. We should love others and count others better than ourselves (Phil. 2:3). Jesus' teaching in the Samaritan story 'love your neighbour as yourself' (Lk. 10:27) is also very related to the golden rule. We should lead a life of service which is committed for the good, welfare and liberation of others.

Golden rule is the summary or the essence of the Bible. We should do to others what we expect from them. It challenges the selfishness, pride, exploitative and oppressive 'mafia' (the attitude that whatever is yours is mine) tendencies. The golden rule implies life of sacrifice, service and 'Gloria' (whatever is mine is yours). It also contradicts the attitude of 'Sophia' (whatever is mine is mine, and whatever is yours is yours). The golden rule is very much found in the life and ministry of Jesus. Jesus incarnated, lived and died on the cross for the sake of humanity which exemplifies the golden rule.

The golden rule also indicates that we are not merely to preach, but to do what we speak about. Doing is important than merely speaking about it. The pragmatic dimension and praxis are given prominence in golden rule. The golden rule is central to the Kingdom of God and the teachings of Jesus.

The concepts such as covenant, agape, kingdom of God and liberation play significant roles in relation to the golden rule. A radical transformation is envisioned by these concepts which are also the thrust of the golden rule. An egalitarian society is the focus of the golden rule. A new world order based on equality and justice is implied in the golden rule.

### (b) Golden Rule a Paradigm for Doing Theology and Ethics

God is transforming, humanizing and liberating the world. Theology and ethics are analytical, reflective, responsive and transformative in their nature. The issues are analysed reflected on and responded to. Not only that, it also challenges what is evil and guides us to transform. An egalitarian society or Christ-centred socialism is advocated by Christianity which condemns the discriminations in the name of race, gender, caste or class. Golden rule looks for non-exploitative, just and humane community. It promotes shalom against war, terrorism and religious fanaticism, and justice against the oppression and inequality.

Love is transformative as it upholds the importance of praxis. The commitment to society is essential in love as in the golden rule. Our faith and praxis should go together. The Christian faith should be rooted in the golden rule. The dialects among the faith, golden rule and the issues are necessary in the development of a theology and ethics. The spirit of liberation is found in the golden rule as it seeks a structural transformation and a total restoration in relationships. It challenges the inhumanity and looks for a humane community in the context of oppression and injustices.

The egoism or selfish interests are questioned by the golden rule. The prophetic consciousness which supports a 'spirituality of combat' is also integral to the golden rule. The feudalistic economic trends like the neo-colonialism found in the form of globalization is challenged by the golden rule as it concentrates on the accumulation of wealth by the powerful few and further marginalizes the poor and the powerless. The golden rule focuses on the empowerment of the poor, victimized and the weaker sections. The 'Koinonia' or the sharing of resources in equitable terms is also on the focus of the golden rule. A fair and just distribution of resources is the solution to all problems. An attitudinal change is essential for a change. Life-affirming and humane values are to be upheld for a transformation which is inherent in the golden rule.

The discriminations of all sorts in the form of caste, gender, race, class and colour should go. In India the *dalits* are undergoing severe suffering. They are the polluted one for the dominant caste. The gender injustice is also very severe in the Indian context. The tribes are suppressed; their resources are exploited and evacuated from their habitat in the name of development. These victimized groups are alienated from the main stream of the society, and their rights and dignity are denied. The golden rule will affirm that all the victimized people are also created by God in His image and their dignity, rights and status are to be upheld. The injustice done to them is a crime against God and humanity. The meaningful participation of all people including the subalterns is to be ensured in the leadership, the decision-making bodies and in the life of the community and nation. If we do not like to be discriminated and dehumanized, why we should do so with the poor and powerless ones?

God's mind is with the oppressed ones, God wants to recognize the dignity and rights of the victimized and marginated and the minorities (Dt. 19:1-13; 20:14; 23:15-16; 24:19-31; Ex. 22:21-24). God has solidarity with the powerless ones as they are created by him. The powerful and dominant have no authority to oppress, exploit and challenge the dignity and rights of the fellow human beings who are powerless. These are found in the understanding of the golden rule.

The Gospel affirms the dignity and rights of the subalterns. Jesus questioned the sabbatical rules which contradicts the golden rule as they are reduced to be instruments of dehumanizing the marginated class while the religious and political leaders and the dominant class of the time have failed to recognize the dignity of the women, poor, the sick ones, the Samaritans and other marginated groups. Jesus loved, healed, restored and liberated them (Mt. 9:27-31; Jn. 5:1-9; 4:5-26; 8:1-11). The golden rule is very much reflected in Jesus' ministry. The golden rule which is reflected in Jesus' ministry is a paradigm for us to do a theology and ethics for liberating the poor, victimized women, *dalits* and tribes. The theology and ethics based on the golden rule is liberative, restoring and humane.

For the ecological concern also the golden rule can play vital roles. An eco-theology or eco-spirituality can be formulated on the basis of golden rule. The ecological crises found in the forms of air, soil and water pollutions, the radiation because of the damage done to ozone layer, global warming, water scarcity, the extinction of the plants and animals (bio-diversity), the diseases like bronchaic problems, cancer and other fatal maladies, and the exhaustion of valuable resources are all the creation of human irresponsibility. The science without humanity or human face is disastrous. The negative effects of the science and technology, the industrialization and the irresponsible forms of developments are doing a tremendous amount of harm to humanity. Human greed is one of the causes for ecological problem. If we had developed a philosophy of life, a value system and theology on the basis of the golden rule, many of these disasters would have been avoided. The philosophies, theologies and ethics that are developed on the basis of selfish interests and capitalistic ideologies have caused the ecological crises as these do not have a concern for others or for the whole of the humanity. These ideologies were self-centred and not other-regarding. A theology and ethics based on golden rule can curb the people from doing injustices to eco-system and help to develop an attitude to preserve the resources and safeguard the creation for the welfare of the whole humanity. The golden rule kindles a vision to withdraw from the violence against the creation.

## Conclusion

The golden rule 'whatever you wish that men would do to you, do so to them' provides inspiration and motivation to shape a life and community in an egalitarian way which would be just, humane, other-regarding and liberative. The '*antyodaya*' and the '*sarvodaya*' (the emancipation of the least and last, and the liberation of all humanity) is possible through the realization of the golden rule. It provides a paradigmatic perspective for doing theology and ethics in the present context.

# 13

# Concern for the Other Sheep

## Mission from the Perspective of the Marginalized

Reaching the 'other sheep' (Jn 10:16) from the perspective of marginalized. This issue is timely, relevant and necessary for mission. I always have the presupposition that we cannot fulfil our mission in India cannot be evangelized unless the *dalits* and tribal people are reached, as they are the major constituent of our nation, India. The concern towards marginalized is a great vision.

### I. The Text and Context of the 'Other'/Other Sheep

John's Gospel is influenced by Judaistic and Greek background. Development of 'Logos' Christology is one of the important elements of this Gospel. John was convincingly presenting Jesus to the Greeks, or non-Jews. John's approach is more inclusive, than exclusive. He transcends the parameters of Judaism. For John, the 'Good news' is meant for the whole people (John 3:16) and salvation is not confined to Jews alone. Gospel is universal in scope, as God is active in all religions and communities.

John 10:16 is fixed in the discourse that belongs to the periscope 10: 7-18. Thus Jesus makes a radical distinction from the Judaistic understanding of 'sheep' and 'shepherd'. There are true shepherd and false shepherds. Jesus referred himself on the true shepherd, and those who came before are referred as thieves (10:8). Jesus said 'I am the gate' (10: 7, 9), 'I am the good shepherd'(10:11). Good shepherd allows people from all communities, and those who enter by him will be saved (10:9). Good shepherd gives life for the sake of sheep and he gives life in abundance (10: 10, 11).

The theme is found in John 10:16. It states, "I have other sheep that do not belong to this hold. I must bring them also, and they will listen to my voice. So there will be one flock, one shepherd."

Here is a specific reference about the inclusive mission of Jesus. The 'sheep' or 'flock' is usually understood as people of Israel. It is a rigid and exclusive view, which alienates the non-Jews or so called gentiles. The Judaistic priestcraft (shepherds) were also not concerned of the non-Jews. But Jesus, the true, good, noble or model shepherd was concerned of the 'other' sheep.

Three main emphases I have found in this passage. They are: 'I have other sheep', 'I must bring them also', and 'there will be one flock'. These indicate God's universal plan of salvation to all people, including the non-Jews and the subalterns or marginated groups. Bruce Milne the message of John, England: IVP, 1993. p. 149) comments in his commentary on the Gospel of John, 'the God who created all people, and who loves all equally, sends the offer of his salvation to all the people of the earth, that all may believe and then unite together in the one great 'flock' of Jesus, the 'good shepherd'. He continues to say that it is a dream captured in the vision of John in Patmos: "after this I have looked, and behold, a great multitude which no man could number, from every nation, from all tribes, and peoples and tongues, standing before the throne and before the lamb' (Rev. 7: 9-10). They cry out 'salvation belongs to our Lord'. Behind Jesus' self-sacrifice there is a unity of all people belonging to all ethnic communities. This is the wider ecumenism, or ecumenical ecumenism as there is unitive vision. All people including *dalits* and tribes are united in Christ.

Jesus' incarnation and self-sacrifice is not merely meant for the few dominant and powerful people, but it was also meant for the poor and powerless. This clearly stated in the Nazareth Manifesto (Lk. 4: 16-21). Jesus came to liberate the oppressed humanity. Jesus sided with poor and marginalized. He has a preferential option for the subalterns.

Jesus told us to make disciple all nations (Mt 28: 18-20). E1, E2, E3 are important over here. Share the good news to our own culture, the culture next to us, and to the distant culture. Mission involves cross-cultural communication. The emphasis of Lausanne conference is also very relevant—'proclaiming the whole gospel to the whole world and to the whole man'. Mission is not limited to our own culture and people, but it is meant for the whole humanity. Mission is related to the whole of creation as there is ecological concerns.

The powerful, dominant and so called superior class, caste and race are always considered. But in the post-modern and post-colonial thinking the powerless, the neglected, the marginalized/ subaltern or the 'other' is considered. The hierarchical and pyramidical structures are questioned which include the capitalism, western dominance, caste and class hierarchy and patriarchy. The 'other' includes the *dalits*, tribal people, blacks, victimized women and the poor. They live in ghettoes. We have in India, the Brahmanic dominance and the dominance of the so called upper class Christians which excludes and dehumanizes the 'other' sheep.

## II. The Condition of the Marginalized

The *dalits* and tribes are the most marginalized people in our country. They are victimized and dehumanized.

### *The Dalits*

According to Poornam Daemel, "nearly 80 per cent of the 100-odd million *Dalits* in India live below poverty line. About 80 per cent *Dalits* are illiterate. Out of the total male landless agricultural labourers, the *Dalits* comprise 48.98 per cent. *Dalit* women constitute 72 per cent of all women agricultural labourers. A large number of urban low-income wage labourers are the *dalits*" (*Emerging Dalit Theology,* edited by Xavier Irudayaraj, p. 37).

The term '*dalit*' in Sanskrit and Hebrew (root word '*dal*') means the same-scattered, crushed or oppressed. They are the early inhabitants of this country, who are of Dravidian stock. It is also observed that there is an Adi-dravida group (proto-Dravidians). The Aryans came later and overpowered and dehumanized them. They use their power and authority over the *Dalits* in the form of Brahmanic dominance. The caste system was instituted based on *Varna* and occupation theory.

The major Dalit groups in India are *chuhras*, *chamars* (U.P. Punjab, Bihar), *malas* and *madigas* (Karnataka and Andhra Pradesh), *Kurvars*, *Sambavas*, and *Chamars* (Thailand and Kerala). Most of the members of these groups are illiterate or less literate and involve in traditional occupations. It is also noted that they only have limited access to wells, roads and temples in some places. The men and women were tortured by high castes, and even their women are raped and forced them to walk naked through the roads as punishment. Most of the *dalits* live in slums, in the unhealthy living conditions. They have no proper shelter, food, employment or health care. The *dalits* in the villages, where they mostly live, are the bond-slaves. They are bonded labourers for the '*janmis*' (land owners) for centuries.

Though Gandhiji said, untouchability is a crime against humanity, this has been practised very much in the Indian context. According to John C.B. Webster, "what Gandhi sought was the purification of Hinduism and Hindus by the removal of untouchability. Gandhi said many times that if Hinduism were to live, then untouchability must go" (*The Dalit Christians: A History*, p. 99).

Gandhiji suggested acts of love and service of *dalits*, but he tried to keep *dalits* in the Hindufold though they are not Hindus. They have a culture and religion of their own, which is different from Vedic-Brahmanic tradition.

The Constitution of India does not allow the status and privileges of *dalits* to *dalit* Christians, though it is provided for Hindus, Buddhists, Jainists and Sikhs. It is intended to stop conversion to Christianity. It is pointed that between ten and fifteen per cent of *dalits* in India are Christians and three-fourth of all Christians in India are *dalits*.

## The Tribal People

The tribal people are the indegenous group who are having a particular geographical area or territory with a distinctive culture. They also have distinct world view, behavioural system and value system. 8 per cent of Indian people are tribes. They are mainly the forest-dwellers. They are the early inhabitants of the land. They constitute around 67.76 million. Their literary rate is around 29 per cent. According to Lokur Commission, scheduled tribes have the following characteristics: (1) primitive traits, (2) distinctive culture, (3) shyness of contact with public at large, (4) geographical isolation, and (5) social and economic backwardness. It is calculated there are over 500 tribes in India and among them 75 are very primitive (N.K. Vaid, *Who Cares for Tribal Development,* pp. 5 ff).

The tribes are denied of their rights, dignity and identity. They are exploited socially, economically and politically. They are forcefully evacuated from their habitat in the name of development. Narmada Valley Andolan is a reaction to such evacuations. They are referred as 'no people' and 'no land' category of people. Though they have a culture of their own, it is unfortunate that they are referred as 'uncivilized' and 'uncultured'. The Sangh Parivar and Brahmanic forces do not want to accept the identity of tribal people, as they want to enlarge their number by calling them 'Hindus'.

The resources of tribal people are tapped by the government machineries and the private sectors. Their land is acquired for the sake of development (e.g. Niyamgiri, Odisha). Their privileges are also snatched away by powerful groups and bureaucracy. They are exploited and undergoing injustice and dehumanization.

## III. Mission to the 'Other Sheep': How to Reach Them

It is important to consider the other sheep. We are happy to share the good news to the dominant groups, but we neglect the marginalized. The significant question is, how to reach the other sheep.

### *1. Acknowledge the Biblical Affirmation with Regard to Marginalized*

God is concerned of the marginalized or subaltern groups (Ex. 3:7, 10; Isa. 58: 6-7; Am. 5:12, 24; Lk. 4:16-21). Bible sides the last, least and the lost (Lk. 19:10; Mt. 9:36). Jesus came to reach or to find out the lost seep. Jesus' incarnation is to integrate the neglected and rejected 'other sheep'. God has solidarity with the victimized people like *dalits* and tribes. Bible shows concern towards aliens, immigrants, refugees, poor and the marginalized. Jesus recognized the Samaritan woman and restored her (John, 4).

### *2. Identify with the 'Other Sheep'*

It is very difficult to identify with the subaltern people. It needs a 'crucified mind' or 'sacrificial mind'. Accepting their identity and living with them are the prerequisites for leading them to Christ.

Jesus was the friend of the poor and marginated. He dwelt among us (Jn. 1:14). He raised the son of Canaanite woman. He identified with the sinners, publicans, Samaritans, the sick and the neglected ones of the society (Mt. 21:31; 9:10). Fr. Damian identified himself with lepers as he lived with them in a sacrificial way. Mother Teresa was the mother of the gettoes. She was concerned of the people in the slums, and those who were rejected in the streets. Once the City Commissioner of Calcutta received a complaint from a person that she was converting people to

Christianity and her 'service' is only a manipulation. In order to inquire about this, the Commissioner took this person also to the house of 'missionaries of charity'. They entered the house and inquired about Mother Teresa. They saw a person dressing a leprosy patient and inquired 'where is Mother Teresa? She replied politely, 'I am Mother Teresa'. They are shocked by the scene. The Commissioner told the complained person, 'This is what she is doing'. They went back with a re-thinking. Jesus was a man for others, according to Bonhoeffer.

Apostle Paul was identifying with the people whom he was serving. He said, 'I have become all things to all people, that I might by all means save some" (I Cor. 9:19-23). He stated, 'I am a debtor both to Greeks and barbarians' (Rom. 1:14).

### *3. Involve in the Transformative/Liberative Mission*

The spiritual regeneration and social transformation are inherent in the gospel. Liberating the oppressed humanity is the mission. Our focus should be a holistic mission. Peace and justice are integral to the kingdom of God. The other sheep is to be integrated, as we liberate them from the domination, oppression and injustice. It is also important to conscientize them, as we make them aware of their present condition and the need for transformation/liberation. The *dalits* and tribal people need a radical spiritual and social change. Literary programmes, health programmes, providing food and shelter, generating employment opportunities, and justice concerns are to be considered to uplift them. Service, development and humanization are essential elements for their transformation.

One of the important thing we should remember is that we should be true to the Gospel, true to ourselves and true to the context. We should be faithful to the calling and sensitive to the issues and do a relevant mission to the context.

We as a team had made a visit to Seethathode, in Pathanamthitta District, where we found a group of tribal people. The first time when the students visited them, they gave some pants and shirts. When I visited later along with the students, I found that these pants are hanging on the trees. They used it once and threw them there, as they are not used to these dresses. They need a *dhoti*, which is relevant to their context. What we offer the people? We should offer a Gospel which is relevant to the marginated people.

***Concluding Remarks***

We should be concerned of the other sheep, the marginated ones, especially the *dalits* and tribes. We have a great and high calling which has a great and significant responsibility. The concern involves our love and compassion, and sacrificing our own life for Christ's sake for the liberation of others. With this calling and commitment, we have to go to different parts of their's country with a distinct and special vision. Our vision is to enlighten the 'other sheep' and to lead them to Christ, our master.

**Conclusion**

The challenge of decolonizing is very crucial to involve in the liberative process. It is important to question the oppressive and dehumanizing forces which makes the life of the poor and subalterns difficult. Everyone born in this earth has the right to have an identity and also to live in dignity with rights. The subalterns are not to live at the mercy of the rich, but they are to be empowered to have a dignified life. It is also our task or mission to have solidarity with the struggles of the suffering people. We have to involve in the process of liberation of the subalterns. We should also work for developing communities of just women and men.

# Index